*Two are better than one,
because they have a good
return for their work.
If one falls down,
His friend can help him up....
Though one may be
overpowered,
two can defend themselves.
A cord of three strands is
not quickly broken.*
   Ecclesiastes 4:9-12

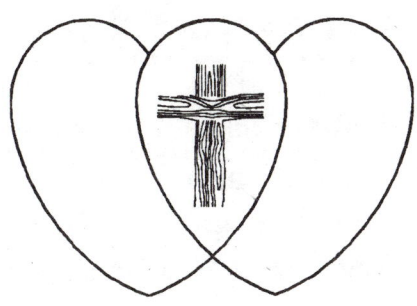

This book belongs to:

_____

RECOMMITMENT VOWS & SONG

VOWS

I _____ love you _____. I promise to unconditionally love you, honor and cherish you all the days of my life. I make this vow before God, knowing I am accountable to Him; and before this assembly as my witnesses. I pledge my loyalty and faithfulness to you and promise to be true to you alone 'til death do us part.

MAKE US ONE

Make us one,
Make us one.
Lord, keep growing us
Together in Your Son.
Our commitment stands
Through the shifting sands;
Lord, teach us to be one.

(sung to tune of HE IS LORD)

GTO FAMILY MINISTRIES

Marriage Enrichment Program

ACHIEVING GOD'S DESIGN FOR MARRIAGE

COUPLES TOGETHER GROWING TOWARD ONENESS

Couple's Guide
(One intended per person)

Harold and Bette Gillogly

Joy Publishing
P.O. Box 827
San Juan Capistrano, CA 92675

ACKNOWLEDGEMENTS

If appreciation came in sizes, we would need the giant economy size to express our thanks to those who helped us put this book together. Peggy Story enthusiastically gave four months of her life to thoroughly edit our first drafts. Neither long hours, hurried dinners or late nights could daunt her pursuit of dangling participles. Her husband Rick and daughter Elisabeth often sacrificed their own comforts to enable Peggy to work so long and hard.

Our artistic abilities would fit in travel size bottles, but we have gracious friends whose artistry would overflow bulk-quantity barrels. Karin Boer drew exquisite illustrations to visually describe what words could not. And Kurt Hartel created and sketched all the cartoons (Kurtoons) throughout both the Couple's Guide and Leader's Guide. These talented and generous friends eagerly donated their gifts to us and to the Lord.

C 1993 Joy Publishing. All rights reserved. No portion of this book may be copied or reprinted without the express prior written permission of Joy Publishing Company, with the exception of portions of the Leader's Guide needed for teaching this program.

Unless otherwise indicated, Scripture quotations used are from The Holy Bible, New International Version of the Bible, copyright C 1978 by the New York International Bible Society. Passages followed by "KJV" are taken from The Holy Bible, King James Version.

Printed in the United States of America.
10 9 8 7 6 5 4 3 2 1

Gillogly, Harold and Bette
Achieving God's Design for Marriage

ISBN 0-939513-84-6

Joy Publishing
P.O. Box 827
San Juan Capistrano, CA 92675

TABLE OF CONTENTS

CHAPTERS

1. COMMUNICATION .... I-1 to I-20
2. THOT-TALK .... II-1 to II-20
3. HOW TO GET A HANDLE ON ANGER. III-1 to III-14
4. FIGHTING FAIR .... IV-1 to IV-12
5. CONSTRUCTIVE CONFLICT .... V-1 to V-20
6. COUPLE DECISION-MAKING .... VI-1 to VI-14
7. ROMANCE & SEX .... VII-1 to VII-30
8. RELATIONSHIP SKILLS .... VIII-1 to VIII-20
9. GOAL SETTING .... IX-1 to IX-6
10. COMMITMENT .... X-1 to X-12
11. SPIRITUAL INTIMACY .... XI-1 to XI-14

APPENDICES

MARRIAGE RELATIONSHIP EVALUATION .... App. A

RECOMMENDED READING LIST .... App. B

GTO RESOURCE ORDER FORM .... App. C

WHAT YOU NEED TO KNOW AT GTO

WELCOME TO GROWING TOWARD ONENESS WEEKEND MARRIAGE ENRICHMENT CONFERENCE!! We know there were great sacrifices made by some of you to get here this weekend. We also know that God is going to **bless** the investment you are making in each other and in your relationship. **Commit** yourself to working with us through the whole weekend, and we're sure that, come Sunday afternoon, you will agree this was one of the best experiences of your life.

RETREAT SETTING (or SEMINAR)

1. IT IS A VERY SCHEDULED WEEKEND -- we're here to work on our relationships with our partners. So please arrive at the sessions on time.
2. NAMETAGS -- please wear them to all sessions for the benefit of those who don't know you.
3. SINGING -- there will be 5 to 10 minutes of singing prior to each session. Show up a little early to enjoy it. Please bring your songsheets to each session.
4. SNACK TABLE -- place your non-spoilable snack on the table provided in the meeting room. Pace yourself as they must last the whole weekend.
5. RECREATION -- Whatever you do during Saturday free time, do it together.
6. DON'T WORRY! NO GROUP DISCUSSION is scheduled for the Romance and Sex session. There will be a question and answer time instead.
7. QUESTIONS FOR ROMANCE AND SEX QUESTION AND ANSWER TIME -- be sure to pick up a few 3 X 5 cards and write out any questions you might have (they may be anonymous). Place them in the wooden box in the back by session time to ensure getting them to us.
8. LEADERS ARE AVAILABLE during break times and free times throughout the weekend to meet with you individually if you desire.

WEEKLY/MONTHLY STUDY SETTING

1. Commit yourselves to working through the entire series. So many topics are covered -- if one doesn't scratch where you itch, another will.
2. The most important part of this series is what happens during your Couple Sharing times. **So don't let anything cheat you out of that!**

The purposes of a man's heart are deep waters, but a man [or woman] of understanding draws them out. (Prov. 20:5)

COMMUNICATION:
AN ESSENTIAL INGREDIENT IN MARRIAGE

I. INTRODUCTION:

Understanding Communication -- the essential ingredients:

A. Definition: Communication is a process (either verbal or non-verbal) of sharing information and/or feelings between two people in such a way that both _____ what is being conveyed.

Many define communication as the transference of information from one to another. But it is much more than that, isn't it? Feelings, as well as information, must be communicated between spouses.

I-1

CHAPTER 1   COMMUNICATION

Understanding of **both** the information and feelings is the goal. But like our little role-play, lots of times we just don't get that far. We think we've communicated--but we haven't.

B. Ingredients:
Communication has these three ingredients:

1. **Words** = About __ of what someone says gets through to us by the words they use. That is, we understand only 7% of what our mates say to us by listening to their words.

2. **Tone** = Tone of Voice comprises __ of what we understand. That is, when our mates talk, to a considerable degree, we perceive what they are saying by the tone of voice they are using.

3. **Non-verbals** = This is the most influencing part of communication with a whopping __ contributing to our understanding. So, the way you look and act when you are saying something to me, directly influences how I understand what you are saying.

C. Listening and Feedback

1. Know why we put "feedback" with "listening"? Because **when we get feedback, we know we are being listened to**. We aren't talking about grunting at the appropriate times. What we are talking about is called the _____ _____.

CHAPTER 1   COMMUNICATION

2. **In listening, we _____ what the other person is saying through our own opinions and needs.** Ordinary tissues can illustrate the filters of my opinions and experiences and needs. I am going to stuff them in my ears. There, now talk to me. How much of what you say to me am I going to understand?

   Objective, careful, unbiased **listening** to our spouses is essential to developing good understanding. So, what do I do with my filters? I am going to have to make a choice to see them for what they are, remove them and listen to my mate **objectively, carefully,** and in an **unbiased** way.

II. UNDERSTANDING THE INGREDIENTS OF BETTER COMMUNICATION

A. Levels of Communication

1. **Level 5 -- _____ --** No risk, nothing of myself, elevator talk

   Here are some examples: "How are you?" "Beautiful weather." "I like your suit."

   This is OK--we need this level of communication. If we really engaged everyone we met, we would be totally overwhelmed and weighed down with everyone's problems.

CHAPTER 1   COMMUNICATION

2. **Level 4 --** _____ -- Telling what we know, information giving. Reporting of facts, but with no personal commentary.

   Here are some examples: "The baby had diarrhea all morning." "The bigwigs from headquarters visited the office today."

3. **Level 3 --** _____ -- Telling what we think.

   Now, we're getting a little deeper. We are sharing ideas and decisions. There is a nominal personal risk, not much, but some. This is where real communication begins.

4. **Level 2 --** _____ -- Telling what we feel.

   This is sharing what we feel about facts, ideas, and judgments. Not the opinions themselves, but how we feel about them.

5. **Level 1 --** _____ -- Complete emotional openness and truthfulness in relationship.

CHAPTER 1 — COMMUNICATION

This is the sharing of hopes, fears, dreams, fulfillments, disappointments and other deep emotions. It is total personal involvement, not just a single fleeting emotion shared.

How about asking your mate sometimes, "What is your greatest need today?" Do you ever ask her or him that question? It could be the start of some great transparent sharing.

B. Why we should seek Transparency

1. We don't seek transparency with _____.

All day long, we interact with people on a very superficial basis. We don't reveal our real selves.

2. Transparency yields _____ _____.

Gen 2:20 -- *So the man gave names to all the livestock, the birds of the air and all the beasts of the field. But for Adam no suitable helper was found.*

Gen 2:25 -- *The man and his wife were both naked, and they felt no shame.* They were naked outside and inside. They had no inhibitions, nothing that hindered their oneness. They had no shame in their bodies, in their minds, nor in their emotions.

It is God's desire that you know the oneness that Adam and Eve shared. He made you to know complete transparency in your marriage, for He intends to take away your loneliness through it. And He has paid for you to have the right to experience that same transparency that Adam and Eve knew. God alone can give you the power to claim that right.

III. ESSENTIAL COMMITMENTS FOR TRANSPARENT COMMUNICATION

A. Make a commitment to express _____. Col. 3:12, 13 -- *Therefore, as God's chosen people, holy and dearly loved, clothe yourselves with compassion, kindness, humility, gentleness and patience. Bear with each other and forgive whatever grievances you may have against one another. Forgive as the Lord forgave you.* Clothe yourself with compassion... Forgive as the Lord forgave you.

1. When we forgive--as we are commanded--**let's express our forgiveness to our spouse.** Say it out loud. And say it with more than words.

CHAPTER 1 — COMMUNICATION

    2. We can say we forgive and NOT forgive--on the other hand, we can forgive and **NOT** express it. Both leave guilt and barriers.

B. Make a commitment to express how you _____.

Psa. 42:4,9,11 -- *These things I remember as I pour out my soul: how I used to go with the multitude, leading the procession to the house of God, with shouts of joy and thanksgiving among the festive throng. I say to God my Rock, "Why have you forgotten me? Why must I go about mourning, oppressed by the enemy?" Why are you downcast, O my soul? Why so disturbed within me? Put your hope in God, for I will yet praise him, my Savior and my God.*

Gal. 6:2 -- *Carry each other's burdens, and in this way you will fulfill the law of Christ.*

    1. You are not being honest with God or yourself or one another if you do not share how you feel.

    2. God is not afraid of our feelings.

CHAPTER 1 — COMMUNICATION

C. Make a commitment to express total _____.

> 1 John 4:10-11 -- *This is love: not that we loved God, but that he loved us and sent his Son as an atoning sacrifice for our sins. Dear friends, since God so loved us, we also ought to love one another.*

> Psa. 103:13-14 -- *As a father has compassion on his children, so the LORD has compassion on those who fear him; for he knows how we are formed, he remembers that we are dust.*

Many times we fail to express acceptance when we unknowingly "shut down" the free expression of feelings our spouse is trying to communicate to us.

1. Ways we reject our mate's feelings:

    a. _____/_____ -- When our mate starts expressing his/her feelings about something we said or did, we react with, "The reason I said that...", "What I meant was..."
    Scriptural Example: Exodus 32:21-24 -- *He said to Aaron, "What did these people do to you, that you led them into such great sin?" "Do not be angry, my lord," Aaron answered. "You know how prone these people are to evil. They said to me, 'Make us gods who will go before us. As for this fellow Moses who brought us up out of Egypt, we don't know what has happened to him.'*

So I told them, 'Whoever has any gold jewelry, take it off.' Then they gave me the gold, and I threw it into the fire, and out came this calf!"

    b. _____ _____ -- Our spouse might start to say that he/she was hurt by something, and we react, "I'm really sorry that...," "I shouldn't have said that...."

Scriptural Example: 1 Samuel 15:24-26 -- *Then Saul said to Samuel, "I have sinned. I violated the LORD'S command and your instructions. I was afraid of the people and so I gave in to them. Now I beg you, forgive my sin and come back with me, so that I may worship the LORD." But Samuel said to him, "I will not go back with you. You have rejected the word of the LORD, and the LORD has rejected you as king over Israel!*

These verses are preceded by a lot of defending and explaining by Saul. His apology is not accepted as sincere by Samuel.

    c. _____ -- Our mate may start to ask why we did something, and our reaction is, "I admit what I did was wrong, but you...", "Well, maybe you're right, but what I can't understand is why you..."

Scriptural Example: Mark 14:66-71 -- *While Peter was below in the courtyard, one of the servant girls of the high priest came by. When she saw Peter warming himself, she looked closely at him.*
"You also were with that Nazarene, Jesus," she said.

CHAPTER 1 — COMMUNICATION

> *But he denied it. "I don't know or understand what you're talking about," he said, and went out into the entryway.*
> *When the servant girl saw him there, she said again to those standing around, "This fellow is one of them." Again he denied it. After a little while, those standing near said to Peter, "Surely you are one of them, for you are a Galilean."*
> *He began to call down curses on himself, and he swore to them, "I don't know this man you're talking about."*

d. _____ -- Our mate may express a feeling of frustration, and we react, "Maybe you should...", "It seems to me that if you..."

Scriptural Example: Job, Chapters 4-11 --
Call if you will but who will answer you?...But if it were I, I would appeal to God: I would lay my cause before him....So hear it and apply it to yourself. (Eliphaz-- chapters 4 & 5)
But if you will look to God and plead with the Almighty, if you are pure and upright, even now he will rouse himself on your behalf and restore you to your rightful place. Ask the former generations and find out what their fathers learned... (Bildad-- chapter 8)

Yet if you devote your heart to him and stretch out your hands to him, if you put away the sin that is in your hand and allow no evil to dwell in your tent, then you will lift up your face without shame....; (Zophar--Chapter 11)

CHAPTER 1   COMMUNICATION

e. _____ -- Our mate starts to express a feeling we don't think is right, or that makes us uncomfortable, so we say, "I don't really see why you feel...," "Gee, honey, there's no need to feel...," "You shouldn't feel like that...."

Scriptural Example: John 12:1-7 -- *Six days before the Passover, Jesus arrived at Bethany, where Lazarus lived, whom Jesus had raised from the dead. Here a dinner was given in Jesus' honor. Martha served, while Lazarus was among those reclining at the table with him. Then Mary took about a pint of pure nard, an expensive perfume; she poured it on Jesus' feet and wiped his feet with her hair. And the house was filled with the fragrance of the perfume.*

But one of his deciples, Judas Iscariot, who was later to betray him, objected, "Why wasn't this perfume sold and the money given to the poor? It was worth a year's wages." He did not say this because he cared about the poor but because he was a thief; as keeper of the money bag, he used to help himself to what was put into it.
"Leave her alone," Jesus replied. "It was intended that she should save this perfume for the day of my burial. You will always have the poor among you, but you will not always have me."

CHAPTER 1   COMMUNICATION

    f. _____ -- Our mates may try to explain a feeling they are having, and we tell them, "What I think you really mean is...," "I don't think you feel..."

    Scriptural Example: Matthew 16:21-23 --
From that time on Jesus began to explain to his disciple that he must go to Jerusalem and suffer many things at the hands of the elders, chief priests and teachers of the law, and that he must be killed and on the third day be raised to life.
Peter took him aside and began to rebuke him. "Never, Lord!" he said. "This shall never happen to you!"
Jesus turned and said to Peter, "Get behind me, Satan! You are a stumbling block to me; you do not have in mind the things of God, but the things of men."

2. Ways we can accept our mate's feelings:

Proverbs 20:5 -- The purposes of a man's heart are deep waters, but a man of understanding draws them out. The purposes of your mate's heart are deep waters, but the husband or wife of understanding draws them out.

    a. _____ -- When our mates try to express how they are feeling, we can say something like, "It sounds as if you feel...," "Guess you really felt...when..."

b. _____ -- We might also say something like, "Are you saying that...?" "I wonder if you feel..."

c. _____ -- As we talk about their feelings for a while, we might say, "I'm not sure what you mean...," "When else do you feel like that? I don't quite understand how you feel about..." Are you saying you're afraid if you do that...?"

d. _____ -- And finally, we might say, "You really felt...Did you also feel...?" "I can see that you feel...If I were in your shoes, I might also feel..." "Do you feel like that?"

(Portions of III.C. were adapted from Lawrence J. Crabb's THE MARRIAGE BUILDER.)

CHAPTER 1   COMMUNICATION

D. **Make a commitment to speak the _____ in _____** -- Ephesians 4:15 -- *Instead, speaking the truth in love, we will in all things grow up into him who is the Head, that is, Christ.* When we are mature, we will speak the truth in love.

The motive for speaking the truth MUST be love!! Don't speak the truth for truth's sake--but for love's sake. This means that sometimes we will just "bite our tongue" and not say what may be the truth because, at the time, it would not be the loving thing to do.

E. **Living Illustrations: Role-plays of Negative/ Positive Communication**

CHAPTER 1 — COMMUNICATION

IV. CONCLUSION

A. Keep all communication lines open

Communication is a three-way proposition, not just a two-way. God is in your marriage too, remember? And you will find that when you are communicating with Him, you are sharing yourselves with one another. It works the other way around too. When you are **not** opening up and sharing yourselves with each other, the communication lines to God will also be strained.

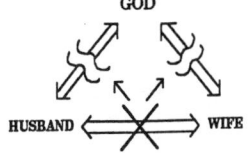

BARRIERS BETWEEN HUSBAND AND WIFE BREAK EACH'S COMMUNION WITH GOD

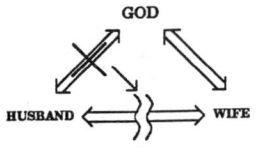

BARRIERS BETWEEN HUSBAND AND GOD BREAK COMMUNION WITH WIFE

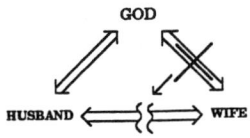

BARRIERS BETWEEN WIFE AND GOD BREAK COMMUNION WITH HUSBAND

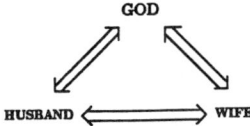

NO BARRIERS PRODUCE OPEN LINES AMONG ALL THREE

CHAPTER 1 COMMUNICATION

B. Sign Marriage Communication Guideline Covenant

Each couple should have a Communication Covenant. This agreement is for you both to read and sign before we go to our small groups. This covenant is in effect for the duration of these meetings. When you sign, you are contracting to follow the listed guidelines while you are at this retreat (or coming to this group). So, read them carefully before you sign, for you will be making promises that God, we and your mate will expect you to keep.

ADDITIONAL NOTES:

CHAPTER 1 — COMMUNICATION

MARRIAGE COMMUNICATION COVENANT

1. I will **listen** and will try not to answer until my mate has finished talking. (Proverbs 18:13 and James 1:13)

2. I will be **slow to speak**. I will try to think first and not be hasty in my words. I will attempt to speak in such a way that my mate can understand and accept what I say. (Proverb 15:23,28; 21:23; 29:20; and James 1:19)

3. I will speak the **truth** to my mate **in love**. I will not exaggerate. (Ephesians 4:15, 25 and Colossians 3:9)

4. I will not use **silence** to frustrate my mate. I will simply explain why I am hesitant to talk at this time.

5. I will not become involved in **quarrels**. I know it is possible to disagree without quarreling. (Proverbs 17:14; 20:3; Romans 13:13; and Ephesians 4:31)

6. I will not respond in **anger**, but will use a **soft and kind** response. (Proverbs 14:29; 15:1; 25:15; 29:11; and Ephesians 4:26, 31)

7. When I am wrong, I will **admit it** and ask for **forgiveness**. (James 5:16)

8. I will not **nag**. (Proverbs 10:19; 17:9; 20:5)

9. I will not **blame** or **criticize** my mate but restore, encourage and edify him/her. (Romans 14:3; Galatians 6:1; and 1 Thessalonians 5:11)

10. If I am verbally attacked, criticized or blamed, I will try not to respond in the **same manner**. (Romans 12:17, 21: 1 Peter 2:23; and 3:9)

11. I will try to **understand** my mate's opinion, allowing him/her to be **different**. I will be concerned about their interests. (Philippians 2:1-4 and Ephesians 4:2)

I hereby agree to try my best to keep these promises throughout this entire marriage enrichment conference.

Signature of Wife _____

Signature of Husband _____

Date _____

CHAPTER 1 COMMUNICATION

V. GROUP SHARING QUESTIONS

1. What are some of the barriers to emotional and transparency levels of communication that couples experience?

2. What are some definite actions that we can take to move toward level one and two communication?

3. Which of the 6 ways of rejecting your mate's feelings do you tend to practice? Which of the 4 ways of accepting your mates feelings do you feel would help you the most if practiced.

CHAPTER 1 — COMMUNICATION

VI. COUPLE SHARING QUESTIONS

1. The following is a survey of your relationship's communication pattern. Fill it out separately--before going over together. It is only for you and your partner's information, so that your communication can grow. So agree not to "blame" or to "defend" while you go over this together.

	NEVER	SELDOM	SOMETIMES	OFTEN	ALWAYS
1. I really listen to you when you talk...					
2. I feel you listen to me...					
3. I understand your NONVERBALS...					
4. We communicate on the "FACT" level...					
5. We communicate on the "OPINION" level...					
6. We communicate on the "EMOTION" level...					
7. We communicate on the "TRANSPARENCY" level...					
8. I accept your feelings...					
9. I feel you accept my feelings...					
10. When I am wrong, I admit it...					
11. When you are wrong, you admit it...					
12. You help me understand my feelings...					

CHAPTER 1   COMMUNICATION

2. Sitting together, have the wife talk about anything she would like to for five minutes. Be sure to time this. During the time she is talking, the husband is to listen and not think about what he will say, nor is he to ask any questions. At the end of the five minutes, he is to repeat back what was said as closely as possible to show he was listening to what his wife was saying. He should also share what he thought she was feeling or what feelings she was expressing.

   After the husband repeats what he can and tells what he heard, the wife responds by telling him whether or not he really heard what she was saying.

   Then husband and wife are to shift roles. The husband is to talk five minutes, the wife to listen and the entire process is to be repeated. Do two more turns if you have time now or do them later.

3. Sit facing each other. Take turns making statements that start with the word "I." Do not make long statements, and do not clarify or ask questions. Simply make the statement and then let your spouse make one. Alternate in this manner for at least ten turns.

   As you go along share more and more of how you FEEL. Examples of how this process might occur is given below:

   "I feel funny sitting down and doing this."

   "I feel that this is going to be different and I am looking forward to it."

   "I wish we could do this more often."

   "I guess I will feel funny letting others know we did something like this."

...we take captive every thought to make it obedient to Christ.
(II Cor. 10:5)

THOT-TALK

I. THOT-TALK AND HOW IT AFFECTS COMMUNICATION

A. Is THOT-TALK a subject we should investigate?
Well, would you say a topic is important if the Bible speaks about it over **300** times? If you do, then the subject we are going to cover in this session is extremely important -- to God and to us. It is so important, in fact, that Proverbs 23:7 states, *"As a man thinks within himself, so is he."* If **what we think** makes us **who we are**, we need to examine very carefully what we think.

CHAPTER 2 — THOT-TALK

1. **What exactly is it?** THOT-TALK is inner _____: messages you tell yourself about yourself, your spouse, your experiences, the past, future, God, etc. They are the thoughts that evaluate facts and events in your life. Sometimes they are clear statements in your mind; sometimes they are merely images or impressions. Whichever kind you have, you're not alone. Everyone talks to themselves.

2. **Here are some truths we don't act like we believe.** There is a very good reason we don't want to believe these truths. They force us to face our personal culpability and responsibility. These truths are:

   a. Most of our _____ (OUR FEELINGS) -- anger, depression, guilt, worry, happiness, sense of well-being, contentment, etc. -- are initiated and escalated by our THOT-TALK.

   b. The way we _____ (OUR BEHAVIOR) toward our spouse is determined by our THOT-TALK -- **not by our mates' behavior.**

   c. _____ we say and _____ we say it (OUR WORDS AND ATTITUDES) are a direct expression of our THOT-TALK.

d. Negative THOT-TALK has at least two things in common:

1) It is almost always _____.

2) It _____ our attention on ourselves, not on our mates or family.

3. We are commanded to think on the _____ -- Philippians 4:8 -- *Finally, brothers, whatever is true, whatever is noble, whatever is right, whatever is pure, whatever is lovely, whatever is admirable--if anything is excellent or praiseworthy--think about such things.*

B. Patterns of negative THOT-TALK and what we can do about them.

Let's explore four common negative **THOT-TALK** patterns. There are others, but these are probably the most common. Do you see yourself in any of the following?

1. _____: This is a **THOT-TALK** pattern in which we think that situations revolve around us.

BIBLICAL ILLUSTRATION: 1 Samuel 18:5-9 -- Saul and David
Whatever Saul sent him to do, David did it so successfully that Saul gave him a high rank in the

army. This pleased all the people, and Saul's officers as well.
When the men were returning home after David had killed the Philistine, the women came out from all the towns of Israel to meet King Saul with singing and dancing, with joyful songs and with tambourines and lutes. As they danced, they sang: "Saul has slain his thousands, and David his tens of thousands."
Saul was very angry; this refrain galled him. "They have credited David with tens of thousands," he thought, "but me with only thousands. What more can he get but the kingdom?" And from that time on Saul kept a jealous eye on David.

RESULTS: We devalue ourselves and _____ _____ from our mates or we _____ them. "What did I do this time? You're always coming home angry, and I pay for it. You just don't love me anymore!" A very tense and angry evening is almost sure to follow.

SOLUTION: _____ the Negative Thought --Substitute Positive THOT-TALK -- **"No, I do not want to think that. It is not true."**

2. _____ **and** _____:
This is a THOT-TALK pattern in which we blow negative events out of proportion and overlook the positive ones.

BIBLICAL ILLUSTRATION: 1 Kings 19:3-18
-- Elijah after Mt Carmel
Elijah was afraid and ran for his life...He came to a broom tree, sat down under it and prayed that he might die. "I have had enough, Lord," he said. "Take my life; I am no better than my ancestors."....
And the word of the Lord came to him: "What are you doing here, Elijah?"
He replied, "I have been very zealous for the Lord God Almighty. The Israelites have rejected your covenant, broken down your altars, and put your prophets to death with the sword. **I am the only one left***, and now they are trying to kill me too."....*
(After the wind, earthquake and fire the still small voice came) When Elijah heard it, he pulled his cloak over his face and went out and stood at the mouth of the cave.
Then a voice said to him, "What are you doing here, Elijah?"
He replied, "I have been very zealous for the Lord God Almighty. The Israelites have rejected your covenant, broken down your altars, and put your prophets to death with the sword. **I am the only one left***, and now they are trying to kill me too."*
(But God answered)...Yet I reserve **seven thousand** *in Israel--***all** *whose knees have not bowed down to Baal and all whose mouths have not kissed him."*

CHAPTER 2   THOT-TALK

RESULTS -- We _____ ourselves or someone else for whatever happened. "I'm not going to do anything with you anymore. You spoiled the whole day by locking the keys in the car. Now what are we going to do? We're stuck! And it's all your fault."

SOLUTION: _____ the Negative THOT-TALK -- Substitute Positive THOT-TALK -- **"No, I do not want to think that. It is not true."**

3. _____ **Thinking and** _____
This is perhaps the sneakiest negative THOT-TALK pattern. We think that we, our mates or our children are either a **total** success or a **total** failure. This causes us to blame our **total** selves or our **total** marriage or mates or children.

BIBLICAL ILLUSTRATION: Genesis 25:29-33; 27:36a -- Esau & Jacob
...Once when Jacob was cooking some stew, Esau came in from the open country, famished. He said to Jacob, "Quick, let me have some of that red stew! I'm famished!" .....Jacob replied, "First sell me your birthright." "Look, I am about to die," Esau said. "What good is the birthright to me?" But Jacob said, "Swear to me

first." So he swore an oath to him, selling his birthright to Jacob.
(Later, when Esau learned that Jacob had also deceitfully taken the blessing that was rightfully his:)
*Esau said, "Isn't he rightly named Jacob? He has deceived me these two times: He **took** my birthright, and now he's taken my blessing!"*

RESULTS: We _____ ourselves. When we fail to see specific behavior as something we **can** change, we do not change. We slip into a downward spiral which ends with our giving up. "I'll never get it right anyway. Why try?" Sometimes we practice this either/or-blame pattern with our spouses and children. As a result, we often leave them feeling hopeless and discounted.

SOLUTION: _____ the Negative Thot-talk--Substitute Positive THOT-TALK -- **"No, I do not want to think that. It is not true."**

4. **Jumping to _____ and _____ reading:** In this THOT-TALK pattern, we tell ourselves what our mates are thinking or feeling.

BIBLICAL ILLUSTRATION: Genesis 12:10-20 -- Abraham and Sarah in Egypt
Now there was a famine in the land, and Abram went down to Egypt to live there for a while because the famine was severe. As he was about

> to enter Egypt, he said to his wife Sarai, "I know what a beautiful woman you are. When the Egyptians see you, they will say, 'This is his wife.' Then they will kill me but will let you live. Say you are my sister, so that I will be treated well for your sake and my life will be spared because of you."

(Pharaoh took Sarai into his palace, but the Lord inflicted diseases on them. So he called Abram in and reprimanded him, giving him back his wife and sending him away.)

RESULTS -- We become _____ or upset with our mates or children for no reason. We can make ourselves depressed or anxious because of some fictitious scenario we painted in our minds, shutting down communication before it has a chance to start. This is a fool proof way of making ourselves and everyone in our house miserable.

SOLUTION: _____ the Negative Thot-talk--Substitute Positive THOT-TALK -- **"No, I don't want to think that. It is not true."**

PERSONAL ILLUSTRATION: I (Harold) had to stay late at work one night, and wanted to let Bette know so she wouldn't worry. (This is a very good practice, men.) When a voice I had often heard disguised as an elderly woman's answered, I knew it was our prankster son playing one of his practical jokes. "Hello," said the feeble voice.

"Adrian, I know that's you. So cut the joke, and let me speak with Mom."

CHAPTER 2

"You must have the wrong number, Young Man."

"This is not the wrong number! Let me speak with Bette. I'm in a hurry to leave here."

"There's no Bette here. You must have the wrong number."

I was rushed and my fuse was short. "This has gone far enough! I want to talk to Bette **NOW**--will you get her for me or not?"

"But there is no Bette who lives here."

I slammed the phone down on the prankster's ear and left work. I fumed all the long way home, growing angrier by the minute. That boy had gone too far this time, and I was going to make him pay for this prank!

I got home, rushed in, slammed the front door, and bounded up the stairs, heading straight for Adrian's room. He pretended to be asleep, but he didn't fool me. "Adrian, you're in big trouble! You went too far with that phone prank!"

"Huh? What? What phone prank?"

"You know good and well what phone prank! Didn't you know I really wanted to talk to your Mom when I called?"

"I haven't answered the phone all night, Dad."

I turned to Bette who had come out into the hallway to see what was happening, and began to spout my tale of woe. "I called this evening to let you know how late I was going to be, and *YOUR* son was playing one of his practical jokes and wouldn't let me talk to you."

With a quizzical expression on her face, she laid her hand comfortingly on my arm. "Honey, our phone hasn't rung all evening."

I was dumbfounded. Somewhere out there was a very upset, innocent old lady. Whoever and wherever she is, I hope she has forgiven me by now.

CHAPTER 2　　　　　　　　　　　　　　　　　THOT-TALK

II. THOT-TALK, ME AND MY PARTNER'S FEELINGS

A. Ways I Reject my Partner's Feelings:

1. _____ / _____ When we personalize or catastrophize, our goal is to avoid handling a negative feeling. So we start explaining why we did such and such. We think things like, *He's going to try to blame this on me. Well, it wasn't my fault.* We just want off the hook, so we say things like..."The reason I said that was...." "What I meant was...."

   Scriptural Example: Exodus 32:21-24 -- Moses said to Aaron, *"What did these people do to you, that you led them into such great sin?" "Do not be angry, my lord," Aaron answered. "You know how prone these people are to evil. They said to me, 'Make us gods who will go before us. As for this fellow Moses who brought us up out of Egypt, we don't know what has happened to him.' So I told them, 'Whoever has any gold jewelry, take it off.' Then they gave me the gold, and I threw it into the fire, and out came this calf!"*

2. _____ _____ Again, we want to be let off the hook. We don't want to admit any mistakes, so our THOT-TALK is, *I don't want to hear this stuff. She always gets upset about everything.* We then say things like, "Oh, I'm sorry...." "I shouldn't have said that. I take it back. Sorry."

   Scriptural Example: 1 Samuel 15:24-26 -- *Then Saul said to Samuel, "I have sinned. I violated the LORD'S command and your instructions. I* *was afraid of the people and so I gave in to them. Now I beg you, forgive my sin and come back with me, so that I may worship the LORD." But Samuel said to him, "I will not go back with you. You have rejected the word of the LORD, and the LORD has rejected you as king over Israel!"*

3. _____: We magnify the bad and attack our mates when they start to express a feeling that might threaten us. We think, *I don't have to put up with this. He's worse than I am.* So we say things like..."O.K. what I did was wrong, but you...." " Well, maybe you're right, but what I can't understand is why you...."

Scriptural Example: Mark 14:66-71 -- *While Peter was below in the courtyard, one of the servant girls of the high priest came by. When she saw Peter warming himself, she looked closely at him.*
"You also were with that Nazarene, Jesus," she said.
But he denied it. "I don't know or understand what you're talking about," he said, and went out into the entryway.
When the servant girl saw him there, she said again to those standing around, "This fellow is one of them." Again he denied it.
After a little while, those standing near said to Peter, "Surely you are one of them, for you are a Galilean."
He began to call down curses on himself, and he swore to them, "I don't know this man you're talking about."

CHAPTER 2 — THOT-TALK

4. _____: We think our mates do some things completely wrong. After all, the only way they could do it totally right is to do it **our** way. So when they express some frustration, we say things like..."Maybe you should do it this way...my way...." "It seems to me that if you would just do it this way...."

Scriptural Example: Job, Chapters 4-11 --
Call if you will but who will answer you?...But if it were I, I would appeal to God: I would lay my cause before him....So hear it and apply it to yourself. (Eliphaz--chapters 4 &5)
But if you will look to God and plead with the Almighty, if you are pure and upright, even now he will rouse himself on your behalf and restore you to your rightful place. Ask the former generations and find out what their fathers learned...(Bildad--chapter 8)
Yet if you devote your heart to him and stretch out your hands to him, if you put away the sin that is in your hand and allow no evil to dwell in your tent, then you will lift up your face without shame. (Zophar--chapter 11)

5. _____: We think in either/or terms, so when our mates try to express feelings of inadequacy, it scares us. We think things like, *You're supposed to meet all my needs. You're the one who should always be strong.* Then we say things like... "You shouldn't feel like that...." "Honey, there's no need to feel...."

Scriptural Example: John 12:1-7 -- *Six days before the Passover, Jesus arrived at Bethany, where Lazarus lived, whom Jesus had raised from the dead. Here a dinner was given in Jesus' honor. Martha served, while Lazarus was among those reclining at the table with him. Then Mary took about a pint of pure nard, an expensive perfume; she poured it on Jesus' feet and wiped his feet with her hair. And the house was filled with the fragrance of the perfume.*
But one of his disciples, Judas Iscariot, who was later to betray him, objected, "Why wasn't this perfume sold and the money given to the poor? It was worth a year's wages." He did not say this because he cared about the poor but because he was a thief; as keeper of the money bag, he used to help himself to what was put into it.
"Leave her alone," Jesus replied. "It was intended that she should save this perfume for the day of my burial. You will always have the poor among you, but you will not always have me."

6. _____: We think we can read our mate's mind better than they can -- or perhaps our mate thinks or talks slower than we do -- so we jump to conclusions and try to tell them what they actually mean. We say things like... ' 'What I think you really mean is....'' ''I don't think you feel...You probably just feel....''

Scriptural Example: Matthew 16:21-23 -- *From that time on Jesus began to explain to his disciples that he must go to Jerusalem and suffer many things at the hands of the elders, chief priests and teachers of the law, and that he must be killed and on the third day be raised to life.*

> *Peter took him aside and began to rebuke him. "Never, Lord!" he said. "This shall never happen to you!"*
> *Jesus turned and said to Peter, "Get behind me, Satan! You are a stumbling block to me; you do not have in mind the things of God, but the things of men."*

We use all these shutdown techniques (even though we didn't really know they were techniques) to protect ourselves from feelings that make us uncomfortable. We're not saying you must be perfect and never use these methods; that would be expecting the impossible. We can't do that either. However, by becoming aware of them, we can work toward rooting them out of our lives.

B. Ways I Accept my Partner's Feelings

Proverbs 20:5 -- *The purposes of a man's heart are deep waters, but a man of understanding draws them out.*

1. _____: If we think...*I'm not going to take what she's saying personally. I'm going to see if I can help her express her feelings completely.* Then we'll say things like...*'*It sounds as if you feel...." "Guess you really felt...when...."

2. _____: If we think...*I'm not going to assume I know what he's trying to say. I'm going to help him say whatever is on his mind.* Then we'll say things like... "Are you saying that...?" "I wonder if you feel...?"

3. _____: If we think...*I'm going to focus on my mate this time. I won't put her down for not being perfect. I'm not perfect either.* Then we'll say things like... "I'm not sure what you mean...." "When else do you feel like that?" "I don't quite understand how you feel about...." "Do you feel _____?"

4. _____: If we think...*This time I'm going to put myself in his shoes and try to understand how he's feeling. It isn't horrible that he feels this way. I'm going to accept his feelings.* Then we'll say things like... "You really felt...Did you also feel...?" "I can see that you feel....If I were in your shoes, I might feel the same way." "Do you feel like that?"

CHAPTER 2 — THOT-TALK

Just as all **The Ways We Reject Our Mate's Feelings** have something in common, so do the four **Ways We Accept Our Mate's Feelings**. Do you know what that is? Once again, it has to do with our focus. When we determine to focus on our mates' needs instead of on our own self protection, wonderful things happen to our communication. It becomes deeper, more genuine and open, kinder and more understanding.

C. **Living Illustrations: Role-plays of Communication with Negative/Positive THOT-TALK.**

III. How to Control your THOT-TALK.

A. **Keep _____ of them:** 2 Corinthians 10:5b -- ...*we take captive every thought to make it obedient to Christ.* Recognize the type of THOT-TALK you are having. Catch yourself at it and take note of what you're telling yourself. If necessary, write down your THOT-TALK each time you become aware of it.

B. **_____ them:** 1 Peter 1:13 -- *Gird up the loins of your mind.* Romans 12:1, 2 -- *Renew your mind.* Challenge them. Bring your thoughts to trial and examine the evidence. The Judge is God and His Word. How does your THOT-TALK measure up to that? If it doesn't conform with what God says, it must be a lie. Throw it out! Say out loud, *No, I don't want to think that. It is not true.* We find it extremely helpful to have a pre-arranged phrase like this on the tip of our tongues. It makes us **ready** to challenge our THOT-TALK.

IV. The Power to _____ Lamentations 3:18-24 -- Jeremiah challenges his negative THOT-TALK and substitutes the positive --

So I say, "My splendor is gone and all that I had hoped from the Lord."
I remember my affliction and my wandering, the bitterness and the gall. I well remember them, and my soul is downcast within me. ***Yet this I call to mind and therefore I have hope:***
Because of the Lord's great love we are not consumed, for his compassions never fail. They are new every morning; great is your faithfulness. ***I say to myself,*** *"The Lord is my portion; therefore I will wait for him."*

A. It is time to _____: Do you want closeness with your mate? Then you must choose it. Do you want an intimate marriage? Then you must choose to take control of your thoughts instead of letting them control you.

1. The choice is mine.

2. I alone am responsible for my choices and behavior.

3. I must be ready to accept the consequences of my choices and behavior.

4. God commands me to capture my thoughts and make them obedient to Him, and He will empower me to obey.

CHAPTER 2 — THOT-TALK

    B. What would happen if:

       1. You chose to _____ your negative **THOT-TALK** when it first starts?

       2. You chose to _____ **on your mate's need to communicate** his/her feelings instead of on your own needs?

       3. You chose to _____ how you feel **in a loving way** instead of sulking and nursing your negative THOT-TALK?

What would happen to your communication and to your emotional oneness?

Would your marriage and your home look different?

ADDITIONAL NOTES:

CHAPTER 2 THOT-TALK

V. GROUP DISCUSSION:

1. How do you think THOT-TALK shapes your attitudes, behavior, feelings and beliefs? Can you give an illustration (positive and negative)?

2. Of the 4 patterns of Thot-talk, which do you tend to practice most?

3. How does THOT-TALK affect the way we reject or accept our partner's feelings?

4. Which steps for controlling and changing your negative THOT-TALK would help you the most?

VI. COUPLE SHARING:

1. I have decided to change my negative THOT-TALK pattern identified in group discussion. I need your help in this process. The ways you could help me turn this negative pattern into positive thot-talk are

   _____

   _____

   _____

2. I know I reject your feelings sometimes by using the six ways talked about in this chapter. I would appreciate your making me more aware of this by _____, because I **do** want to accept your feelings.

3. I would sense you were accepting my feelings more if you practiced: (circle one) Reflecting, Clarifying, Exploring, Extending. Here's an illustration of how that would help me:

   _____

   _____

   _____

[Love] is not rude ... it is not easily angered.... (I Cor. 13:5)

HOW TO GET A HANDLE ON ANGER

I. INTRODUCTION

ANGER IS THE MAJOR CAUSE OF MARRIAGE FAILURES today because it alienates husbands and wives. So declares David Mace, who has over fifty years of marriage counseling experience. The problem is not that anger happens in marriage -- but that we don't know how to **handle** our own anger nor the anger of our mates. **We mis-use anger.**

II. REVIEW OF KINDS OF ANGER

A. Righteous Anger	vs.	Sinful Anger
1. Unselfish		1. Selfish
2. Always controlled		2. Often uncontrolled
3. Directed toward the act		3. Directed toward person
4. Has no resentment		4. Harbors bitterness and resentment/ retaliation
5. Maybe ___ of our anger		5. Probably ___ of our anger

These percentages aren't clinical. We didn't get them from a survey. They simply reflect our observations of others and ourselves. Be honest, though, aren't they about right? The bulk of our experience is with sinful anger -- therein lies our problem. We need to

CHAPTER 3   HANDLING ANGER

investigate anger so that we can get a handle on it. Then maybe it won't handle us so much.

B. How Sinful Anger affects us. Selfish anger is not a harmless emotion. Make no mistake, when we nurse anger we **suffer its consequences** in our lives: bodies, minds and spirits. Here are just a few results of anger in our lives.

1. **It becomes a _____: the more we are angry, the more we become angry.** Proverbs 22:24-25 says, *Do not make friends with a hot-tempered man, do not associate with one easily angered, or you may **learn his** ways and get yourself **ensnared**.* Anger is a trap because it is a habit, a **learned habit**.

   [margin: habit]

2. **It reduces our ability to _____ clearly.** Proverbs 14:17a -- *A quick tempered man does foolish things.* Anger robs us of our perspective.

   [margin: Think / Reason]

3. **It upsets the chemical balance of our bodies and can cause _____ _____:** Proverbs 12:18 says, *Reckless words pierce like a sword, but the **tongue of the wise brings healing**,* healing to the one who speaks **and** the one who listens. THYROID, MIGRANES,

   [margin: Physical illness]

4. **It pushes the _____ we love away from us.** Proverbs 25:24 -- *Better to live on a corner of the roof than share a house with a quarrelsome*

   [margin: People]

wife [or husband]. Do you enjoy being around an angry person? Of course not! Then do **you** want to be the one other people avoid?

[margin note: ANGER]

5. **It makes the people we love angry at us.**
   _____ **begets anger.** Proverbs 15:1 -- *A gentle answer turns away wrath, but a harsh word stirs up anger.* When we act angrily, we ignite our mates' defense systems. The scripture is true. When we act and speak harshly, we trigger our mates' and children's anger.

[margin note: example]

6. **It gives my family a poor _____ that will effect my children, grandchildren and generations to come.** Leviticus 26:39b-40, and 42 -- *...because of their fathers' sins they will waste away. But if they will confess their sins and the sins of their fathers...I will remember my covenant with Jacob....*

The bottom line is that **selfish anger does not do ONE positive thing** for me, my spouse, my children or for anyone else around me!

III. **The truth about anger**: Here are six truths about anger. If we truly believe these truths and act upon them, we will take a **giant step** toward handling our anger.

[margin note: should]

A. **We get angry because real life is not the way we think it _____ to be.** Psalm 37:8 -- *Refrain from*

CHAPTER 3   HANDLING ANGER

anger and turn from wrath; ***do not fret*** *-- it leads only to evil.*

[margin note: Feeds / increases]

B. Expressing your anger does not lessen your anger. It usually _____ it. Proverbs 30:33c -- *...stirring up anger **produces strife**.*

[margin note: Learned]

C. How you deal with your anger was _____. Ephesians 4:22-24 -- *You were taught, with regard to your former way of life, to **put off your old self**, which is being corrupted by its deceitful desires; to be made new in the attitude of your minds; and to **put on the new self**, created to be like God in true righteousness and holiness.*

[margin note: Responsible / You]

D. Your partner is not _____ for making you angry. _____ are. Matthew 5:22a -- *But I [Jesus] tell you that anyone who is angry with his brother will be subject to judgment.*

[margin note: Secondary]

E. Anger is a _____ emotion. It is a symptom that indicates something else is happening inside us. Anger is actually a **response to another emotion** we are feeling.

III - 4

CHAPTER 3   HANDLING ANGER

FEAR

1. _____ -- We might be afraid our partners will over-ride us, control us, verbally attack us, ignore us, or disagree with us. To protect ourselves from that **fear**, we attack in anger.

   INSECURE

   Red Flag Question: Fear often erupts into expressions of anger in dramatic ways. When we **burst** into anger, we'd better ask ourselves: "Is there something **I'm afraid of** right now?"

HURT

2. _____ -- The second primary emotion usually found under anger is hurt. Many things can hurt us: a sharp word, lack of appreciation, or our mate's forgetfullness about something important to us. We usually don't even recognize that it **is** hurt we are feeling because we so quickly cover it with anger. *UN-APPRECIATED*

   Red Flag Question: The red flag questions this time are; "Am I feeling hurt? **What is hurting me?**" You must recognize and deal with the hurt in order to manage the anger.

Frustration

3. _____ -- When things don't go the way we want, or the way we think they "ought to," we get frustrated. Or when confronted with a problem we can't solve, we get frustrated. There are, of course, a lot of little annoyances and quirks about our mates that **we can not solve or control**; that's why they trigger such frustration in us.

CHAPTER 3 — HANDLING ANGER

> **Red Flag Question:** "Why am I frustrated? What am I doing to **frustrate myself**?" We can see only one good solution to frustration: give your partner (and other people and circumstances) permission to be different from what you expect. Allow your spouse the freedom to be him or herself. It is foolish to fret over things you cannot control. Remember Psalm 37:8? *Don't fret -- it leads only to evil*...evil for ourselves, as well as evil for others.

F. _[BLAME]_____ **fuels the fires of anger.** Proverbs 27:4a -- *Anger is cruel and fury is overwhelming.*

1. **We blame our mates thinking that we can _[improve]_____ them.** What a useless and self-defeating pursuit! Does being blamed make **you** straighten up and become a nicer person? Does it make **you** want to change for the better? **Blame does not work...it overwhelms**.

    a. **When we blame, we _[trigger]_____ our partner's self-defense system.** Proverbs 17:14 says, *Starting a quarrel is like breaching a dam; so drop the matter before a dispute breaks out.*

    b. **When we blame, it keeps our anger _[going]_____.**

    c. **When we blame, it distracts us from discovering a _[solution]_____ to our frustration.**

III - 6

CHAPTER 3 — HANDLING ANGER

2. The solution? Ephesians 4:32 -- *Be kind and compassionate to one another, forgiving each other, just as in Christ God forgave you.*
_____ **releases us** from the pressure of making our mates PAY for what they have done to us.

(margin note: Forgiveness)

IV. RESPONSES TO ANGER

A. The ways that _____ _____ -- The Deadly R's.

(margin note: don't work)

1. Repression -- _____ **our anger** leads to resentment (another deadly **R**). Ephesians 4:26-27 -- *In your anger do not sin. Do not let the sun go down while you are still angry, and do not give the devil a foothold.* Anger here means *resentment*, that slow burning anger we try to keep well hidden.

(margin note: Swallows)

CHAPTER 3 — HANDLING ANGER

    a. Lie #1 -- Anger is _____ [sin] ...so if I'm a good Christian, I shouldn't get angry.

    b. Lie #2 -- Being angry always means _____ [loosing control]: yelling and stomping your feet, etc., so if I don't do that, I'm controlling my anger. Being a nice person is better than yelling. People who express their anger are not nice. But I'm a nice person.

    c. Results:

        (1) We _____ [store up] the pressure like air in a balloon until it finally bursts. Carrying all that pressure around can make us bitter fault-finders. Hebrews 12:15 -- *See to it that no one misses the grace of God and that **no bitter root grows up to cause trouble** and defile many.*

        (2) Our anger _____ [oozes] out in subconscious ways: burning dinner, having a headache at bedtime, avoiding people, pouting, teasing, sarcasm, silence, gossip, or even depression.

2. Expression -- Rage. _____ [Uncontrolled] anger. This is the other deadly **R**. Proverbs 29:11 -- *A fool gives full vent to his anger, but a wise man keeps himself under control.*

    a. Lie #1 -- If I _____ [vent] my anger, I can get it off my chest and everything will be fine.

    b. Lie #2 -- I _____ [yell] when I'm angry. That's just the way I am; I can't change. Besides, I have a right to punish people who don't meet my expectations.

CHAPTER 3 — HANDLING ANGER

    c. Results -- Rage is like open warfare because it blows up the bridges between us. If we blow up too many bridges, how will we connect? We alienate our mate when we express anger uncontrollably. Couples become polarized, living in two separate worlds, hurting and being hurt. Scripture commands us to remove this response to anger from our lives. Ephesians 4:31 -- *Get rid of all bitterness, rage and anger, brawling and slander, along with every form of malice.*

B. The ways that _____ *[work]*

1. _____ it -- admit your anger, but keep your emotions under control. Proverbs 19:11 -- *A man's wisdom gives him patience; it is to his glory to overlook an offense.* Ah, you knew there was a catch to it. It's going to take work! *[control]*

2. _____ it -- Admit your anger, control it, then explore it to discover its **cause**. Remember, there is fear, hurt or frustration under that anger. These are the emotions that need attention. Only by dealing constructively with the **root cause(s)** of our anger can we find a **long term solution**. *[Process]*

   Here are 6 steps in processing anger:

   a. _____ **to** _____ **the moment we begin to feel angry.** Say it **out loud** immediately. This will keep us from holding on to angry, resentful thoughts. *[contract to confess]*

CHAPTER 3   HANDLING ANGER

agree

b. _____ **to not attack.** It is important that we not attack each other in anger. To achieve this -- yes, it is possible -- we simply need to agree to **control our angry responses.** We don't need to attack, because we know there is a better way. We must **refuse to hold thoughts of retaliation.** Romans 12:18 commands, *If it is possible, as far as it depends on you, live at peace with everyone.*

Review + Rehearse

c. _____ **and** _____. After a **cooling off** period, **review** the situation that caused the anger, not with blame but with mutual concern. Then **rehearse** what you will do when a similar situation occurs in the future. In other words, it is possible for you to plan your behavior changes as a couple.

Illustration: A while back, it seemed we got into an argument whenever Bette was driving. After one such heated ride, we did some **R and R** (Review and Rehearse). We discovered that the root of Bette's anger was my (Harold's) constant driving instructions: "get over in the next lane," "turn left up here," "don't stay in back of this truck, I can't see around it." She felt I was treating her like I thought she couldn't drive. And I admit, I had fallen into a bad habit of "back seat driving." We **reviewed what was happening** in our anger pattern and **why**.

Then we **rehearsed** what we would do in the future to dismantle that anger pattern. Bette suggested that I precede my helpful suggestions with a simple, "Need my help?" She would then have the option to reply, "Yes, help me," or, "No, thank you." This sounded reasonable to me, so we gave it a try.

It worked! What **was** an anger pattern in our relationship is **now** something we laugh at. I still forget once in a while and start to "back seat drive," but I usually catch myself in time to interrupt with, "OOPS, I mean, do you need my help?" Are there some patterns of anger you would like to remove from your relationship? Try some **R and R.**

d. **Choose to _FORGIVE_.** We all blow it sometimes. We can not meet all our mates' expectations, nor they ours. However, when our partners fail, **we can choose to forgive** them.

Colossians 3:13 -- *Bear with each other and forgive whatever grievances you may have against one another. Forgive as the Lord forgave you.*

CHAPTER 3 — HANDLING ANGER

    SUPPORT

    e. Seek _____. We all need help from the Lord and from others. Immerse yourself in God's Word. Meditate on passages about how to handle anger. Pray. The Lord is eager to help you; He's waiting for you to ask. Tell Him you're ready to start obeying His commands about anger.

    COVENANT

    f. _____ to Change. When we ask our partner for help, our anger becomes a problem to solve together instead of a wall of alienation between us. We can make a covenant to help each other change and grow out of our anger.

V. GOD'S PROMISE

_____ (Prov. 29:11b)
And will help you keep yourself under control.

_____ (Prov. 19:11b)
It will make you able to overlook offenses

_____ (Prov. 19:11a)
And wisdom, in turn, will give you patience

_____ (Prov. 19:20b)
That will make you wise.

_____ (Prov. 19:20a)
Listen to advice and accept instruction

CHAPTER 3   HANDLING ANGER

James 3:17-18 -- *But the wisdom that comes from heaven is first of all pure; then peace loving, considerate, submissive, full of mercy and good fruit, impartial and sincere. Peacemakers who sow in peace raise a harvest of righteousness.*

VI. GROUP DISCUSSION

1. Of the six things sinful anger does to me, the most detrimental is _____ because _____.

2. Of the six truths about anger, the most difficult for me to accept is _____ because _____. The most helpful for me is _____ because _____.

3. Of the three primary emotions that are at the root of anger (fear, hurt and frustration), the one that causes most anger is probably _____.

4. Talk about each of the steps for handling anger. Can you give illustrations of each step?

VII. COUPLE SHARING

1. I am naturally a (1) repressor or (2) expresser. I often respond to my anger by _____.

2. In the past, I have tended to become angry with you over _____. I think my underlying feeling is _____ (hurt, fear, frustration). I confess this is wrong and take responsibility for my anger. Will you forgive me?

3. You could help me recognize and confess my anger by

   _____

   _____.

4. I enlist your help when you see that I am becoming angry. To help me, please give this signal: _____.
   I agree to this plan of action, and I have no right to be angry when you practice it.

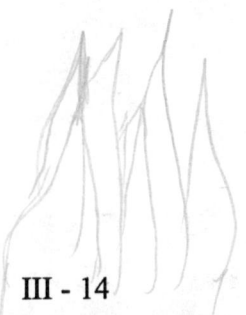

Make every effort to keep the unity of the Spirit through the bond of peace. (Eph. 4:3)

FIGHTING FAIR THE ONLY WAY TO FIGHT

I. INTRODUCTION--AGREE/DISAGREE STATEMENTS

Place a check mark indicating whether you agree or disagree with statements 1-14. No fence-riding -- you must either **agree** or **disagree**. So define the terms in your own mind and take a position on each statement.

AGREE DISAGREE

_____   _____   1. When fighting, we should tell the truth even if it hurts our spouse.

_____   _____   2. When people become angry in their fights, they lose control.

_____   _____   3. Fighting should be postponed when one or the other spouse is tired.

_____   _____   4. When you criticize your mate in the heat of a fight, make sure it's constructive.

_____   _____   5. Sometimes it is O.K. to yell in order to get your point across in the heat of a fight.

_____   _____   6. To bring a disagreement to a head, you may need to confront your spouse in public.

CHAPTER 4   FIGHTING FAIR

_____ _____ 7. You can not finish a fight without forgiveness.

_____ _____ 8. We fight over symptoms, not actual causes.

_____ _____ 9. Fights should never deal with more than one issue at a time.

_____ _____ 10. When categorizing or name-calling during a fight, you must make certain you are accurate.

_____ _____ 11. Bringing up the past *can* be helpful in settling today's fights.

_____ _____ 12. Quoting well-known authorities on the subject *can* give your side of the argument credibility.

_____ _____ 13. When your partner finally gives in, you know you have won the fight.

_____ _____ 14. Physical contact while fighting should be avoided because of our human tendency to inflict hurt when we are angry.

II. GUIDELINES FOR FIGHTING FAIR

1. **Keep it _____.** The Agree/Disagree statement was, "When fighting, we should always tell the truth even if it hurts our spouse." Ephesians 4:25 -- *Therefore each of you must put off falsehood and speak truthfully to his neighbor, for we are all members of one body.* It **is** essential that we commit ourselves to an honest relationship, so that we avoid the trap of acting or lying just to win over our partner. However, we must be tactful and speak the *truth in*

love (Ephesians 4:15). If we speak the truth for truth's sake, we might say things which deeply hurt our mates. That's why God qualifies truth "with love." He wants us to **build each other up**, not tear each other down, even in the name of truth.

2. Keep it under _____. The Agree/Disagree (from now on, we'll refer to it as A/D) statement number 2 was, "When people become angry in their fights, they lose control." Ephesians 4:26a -- *In your anger, do not sin.* Proverbs 29:11 -- *A fool gives full vent to his anger, but a wise man keeps himself under control.*

Chapter 5 taught a lot about anger and the control of our natural responses to it -- both repression and expression. You know as well as we do that it is essential to keep our reactions under control and to refrain from using **deadly weapons** on each other. Deadly weapons are words that trigger immediate defense: words like "always," "never," "You...," "If you really loved me..." Our simple rule is: always avoid using "always," never say "never," and leave the rest of the deadly weapons alone!

3. Keep it _____ _____. The A/D statement was, "Fighting should be postponed when one or the other spouse is tired." Ephesians 4:26b-27 -- *Do not let the sun go down while you are still angry, and do not give the devil a foothold.* The principle of this verse is to handle anger in a **timely manner**. It **can** mean we agree not to go to sleep before a fight is settled. Or it **can** mean we deal with it enough to mitigate some of its sting and agree to settle it later -- in the morning or the earliest available time. Some of us can't sleep when we're angry, but many of us get so punchy at night that we couldn't settle a fight if our lives depended on it. We must mutually agree on how we as a couple will finish conflicts that drag on. But **when** we handle our fights is not as important as our mutual agreement **to** handle them in a timely manner, so the devil can **not** gain a foothold in our relationship.

4. Keep it _____. The A/D statement: "When you criticize your mate in the heat of a fight, make sure it's constructive." Should we ever criticize our mate -- whether we're in a fight or not? Does criticism have a legitimate place in a Christian marriage? To criticize means "to judge, to find fault, to censure." That sounds suspiciously like blame, doesn't it? And, like blame, it is counterproductive.

Even with "constructive criticism," we must watch our motives carefully. We're often **quick** to criticize (even constructively), and **slow** to forbear the shortcomings of our mates. Colossians 3:12-13 -- *Therefore, as God's chosen people, holy and dearly loved, clothe yourselves with compassion, kindness, humility, gentleness and patience. **Bear with each other** and forgive whatever grievances you may have against one another.*

Ephesians 4:28 -- *He who has been stealing must steal no longer, but must work, doing something useful with his own hands, that he may have something to share with those in need.*

CHAPTER 4   FIGHTING FAIR

5. **Keep it _____.** The A/D statement: "Sometimes it is O.K. to yell in order to get your point across in the heat of a fight." Ephesians 4:29 -- *Do not let **any unwholesome talk** come out of your mouths, but **only what is helpful** for building others up according to their needs, that it may benefit those who listen.*

We must watch our words and guard our tone. The louder our voice, the less our mate will hear; the uglier the words, the less we will communicate. Want to get someone's attention? Whisper. It works even in a third grade classroom.

6. **Keep it _____.** A/D statement number 6: "To bring a disagreement to a head, you may need to confront your spouse in public." Proverbs 13:3 -- *He who guards his lips guards his soul, but he who speaks rashly will come to ruin.* Ephesians 4:31 -- *Get rid of all bitterness, rage and anger, brawling and slander, along with every form of malice.* Never, never, never embarrass your mate in public. Whether an open potshot or a subtle "joke," verbal swings taken in public hurt much more deeply than private wounds.

If you were reared in a family who teased each other unmercifully, we implore you to keep in mind that you **can not** treat your wife or husband the way you do your sister or brother. Too much of your mate's self esteem depends on **you**.

7. **Keep it _____ ____.** The A/D statement was: "You can not finish a fight without forgiveness." Ephesians 4:32 -- *Be kind and compassionate to one another, forgiving each other, just as in Christ God forgave you.* The fight is over when forgiveness has been asked for and given. **Don't assume** everything is all right again. **Make sure** everything is all right again. Then you won't be burying "ghosts" that will come back to haunt you.

   Notice -- we are to forgive *just as in Christ God forgave you.* How **does** God forgive us? He forgives completely, with no remembrance of our sin. He *hurls all our iniquities into the depths of the sea* (Micah 7:19). Cory Ten Boom used to add in her thick Dutch accent, "And then, Beloved, He puts up a NO FISHING sign." He never brings them back up to hold over our heads. How does He **do** that? He **chooses** to do that! He chooses to **thoroughly forgive**, and He expects us to do the same.

8. **Find out _____ you're fighting about.** A/D statement number 8: "We fight over symptoms, not actual causes." Proverbs 18:15 -- *The heart of the discerning acquires knowledge; the ears of the wise seek it out.* In Chapter 5, we discussed how anger is a secondary emotion, and stressed the importance of discovering the feelings below the surface. This Scripture tells us that we are **wise** if we **seek to discern** the **underlying cause** of our -- and our mate's -- anger. If what starts things off is usually only the **symptom**, not the cause, then we need to *seek out* the **cause**.

CHAPTER 4　　　　　　　　　　FIGHTING FAIR

9. **Stick to the _____.** The A/D statement: "Fights should never deal with more than one issue at a time." Usually, this is true. We won't settle anything if one or both of us say things like, "And that reminds me...." If there are several issues disturbing us, we need to deal with one at a time. Throwing everything at our mate in one discussion just to get them off our chest **does not work**. We can overwhelm our mates and ourselves. None of us can deal with five problems at the same time. It seems hopeless. But **one** problem at a time? **That** we can handle.

10. **Avoid _____ or name calling.** The A/D statement was, "When categorizing or name-calling during a fight, you **must** make certain you are accurate." Matthew 5:22c -- ...*anyone who says, "You fool!" will be in danger of the fire of hell.* Sometimes we say things in the heat of an argument like: "You're just saying that because you're a woman." "You men are all alike." "You're just like

your mother!" Ooh, even if what we say is accurate, **name calling is deadly**. It's a habit we must avoid. And those who already have gotten into this habit need to break it as quickly as possible.

11. Leave out past _____. A/D statement number 11: "Bringing up the past *can* be helpful in settling today's fights." 1 Corinthians 13:5 -- *[Love] is not rude, it is not self-seeking, it is not easily angered, it **keeps no record of wrongs**.* If we've burned the Stamp Books we spoke of in guideline 9, then there will be no past histories to bring up. If we've truly settled yesterday's conflicts, then they're gone, **never** to be brought up again.

There is a time, however, when past fights **must** be brought up -- when they **were not** settled the first time. Even then, they must be brought up for **one reason** only -- so that they **can** be settled. Old conflicts are like chains. The longer we carry them around, the heavier they get. We don't have to carry them any longer. We can lay them down; settle past wrongs; and get on with today.

Here's what the Apostle Paul had to say about how we should handle the past: *Brothers, I do not consider myself yet to have taken hold of it [becoming like Christ]. But one thing I do: **Forgetting what is behind and straining toward what is ahead,** I press on toward the goal to win the prize for which God has called me heavenward in Christ Jesus. All of us who are mature should **take such a view of things.*** (Philippians 3:13-15a)

CHAPTER 4   FIGHTING FAIR

12. **Don't allow _____ parties.** A/D statement: "Quoting well known authorities on the subject **can** give your side of the argument credibility." Don't bring in Dr. Dobson, Dr. Ruth or even your mother to support your position. Just fight it out on your own. If you keep in mind that you have **no other option** but to settle your conflicts, you **will find solutions** you can live with. By the way, it's only fair to warn you: if you use **us** to back up your position, we'll track you down.

13. **Remember it's the one you _____ you're fighting with.** The A/D statement for this guideline was, "When your partner finally gives in, you know you have won the fight." 1 Corinthians 13:5 -- *[Love] is not rude, it is not self-seeking....* Why do we have a driving need to win? Why do we believe so fervently we are right and our partners are wrong? James 4:1-2 explains our problem. *What causes fights and quarrels among you? Don't they come from your desires that battle within you? You want something but don't get it.* We are out to win, even if we must step on our mates to do so. We fail to realize that when we win this way, we **lose**. We **both** lose.

14. **Hold _____ while fighting.** The final A/D statement was, "Physical contact while fighting should be avoided because of our human tendency to inflict hurt when we are angry." When we have conflict, our natural tendency is to retreat from one another. We feel alienated from our partners, because we believe they must not love us as much as they say. Otherwise they wouldn't treat us like this. Our real need during conflict, however, is the complete opposite of our usual behavior.

We **need** touch. Touching reminds us that **WE** are more important than any issue. And as you will discover, it is difficult to fight while touching. The trick in following this guideline is to make a mutual decision to hold hands during your next fight...but make this decision now while you're **not** fighting. You can't wait until an argument has started, and then remember, "Oh, we were supposed to decide to hold hands." By then, it's too late. So why not decide today to give it a try?

CHAPTER 4 — FIGHTING FAIR

VI. GROUP DISCUSSION

1. Are any of these guidelines new to you?

2. Which guideline do you feel is the most difficult to apply? Why?

3. Which **three** guidelines do you feel would be the most helpful to you in fighting fairer?

4. Which one of these three will you need the most help in applying?

CHAPTER 4   FIGHTING FAIR

VII. COUPLE SHARING

1. The guideline I will need the most help in applying is _____. You have my permission to help me apply this by

   _____.

2. The guideline I would most like you to apply in our fights is _____.

3. Review the 14 guidelines together asking each other the following questions about each one:

   (1) Do we need this guideline in our fighting?

   (2) Are we applying this one regularly?

   (3) Do I need to concentrate on this one as one of my top three guidelines?

   (4) Do I need help in applying this one? Will you help me by _____?

Be kind and compassionate to one another.... (Eph. 4:32)

CONSTRUCTIVE CONFLICT

I. INTRODUCTION: Conflict alienates couples, so how can it become constructive?

II. WHAT IS CONFLICT?

If we obeyed -- **really obeyed** -- two simple verses in Scripture, we would have **very little conflict** in our homes. These two verses describe what conflict is made of and how to rid ourselves of it. What are these miracle verses? Ephesians 4, verses 31 and 32 -- *Get rid of all bitterness, rage and anger, brawling and slander, along with every form of malice. Be kind and compassionate to one another, forgiving each other, just as in Christ God forgave you.*

A. _____ = **the harboring of hurts, disappointments, rejections and unresolved conflicts.**

B. _____ **(or wrath) = a temper flare up which causes us to act without considering the consequences.**

CHAPTER 5 — CONSTRUCTIVE CONFLICT

C. _____ = a strong response of irritation; an abiding condition of the mind, frequently with a view to taking revenge.

D. _____ (or clamor) = a response without regard for the feelings of our mates; the tumult of controversy.

E. _____ = a response intended to defame and show contempt; verbal abuse.

F. _____ = spite and ill-will; resentment which holds a grudging desire to see our mates suffer.

God urges us to *get rid* of these six traits from our lives. Perhaps you are thinking, "Well, when God said that, He hadn't met MY spouse!" Sorry. If any or all of these are a part of our lives, we **can not blame our spouses**. **We are responsible** for our own thoughts and behavior **regardless** of how our partners act. You probably find it as hard as we do to accept this truth. The commands in verse 32 won't be much easier, but we'll save that for later. First, we need to explore Conflict a little more.

CHAPTER 5   CONSTRUCTIVE CONFLICT

III. WHY WE HAVE CONFLICT

A. _____

We fight for three basic reasons. The first is our differences. Differences cause a great deal of conflict because **we are different**.

1. The Differences that can lead to Conflict:

   a. We are different because of the way we were _____. Our families of origin were different. One mate's parents might have been strict, while the other's were lenient. One's family might have made a big deal about birthdays and holidays, but the other's didn't. Our families probably handled anger and problem-solving in unique ways, and used different methods of child-rearing. They may even have had conflicting value systems.

   b. We are different because of our _____ _____. Every child born into a family is actually born to a different family. Hold on...let us explain. The first born comes into a family of two, usually inexperienced, adults. The second born enters a family of two more experienced adults and one sibling. The third child is born into a family of two tired adults and two siblings. Family dynamics change with the addition of each child.

   c. We are different because some of us are _____ and some are _____. Thinkers use details and logic to form their conclusions and want their feeler mates to logically express what they **think** about things. Feelers process information through their emotions and want their thinker mates to express how they **feel** about things.

d. We are different because some of us are _____ and some are _____ people.
Inner people are introspective and thorough, but rarely the life of the party. Outer people are gregarious and open in their communication, but often fail to think everything through carefully. If inner and outer people focus on each other's weaknesses, they become irritated. If, however, they focus on each other's strengths, they realize they need each other. They **complement** one another.

e. We are different because some of us are _____ and some are _____. Organized people like to plan their lives down to the hours and minutes. Spontaneous people enjoy letting life simply happen to them. Organized people are usually steady and dependable, while spontaneous people are usually flexible and fun.

f. We are different because some of us are _____ and some are _____. You noticed? This in itself accounts for huge differences. Our bodies are different, both in looks and function. We tend to express our emotions in different ways. We even process thoughts differently. We are gloriously different! Although God could have made Eve a **clone** of Adam, He chose to make her the **complement** of Adam.

CHAPTER 5 — CONSTRUCTIVE CONFLICT

This list is from Joe Taunebaum's book, <u>Male and Female Realities</u>.

MEN THINK WOMEN SHOULD:	WOMEN THINK MEN SHOULD:
1. Talk less	1. Talk more
2. Be less emotional	2. Be more emotional
3. Be more physical	3. Be less physical
4. Be less romantic	4. Be more romantic
5. Be more sexual	5. Be less sexual
6. Be less involved with others	6. Be more involved with others
7. Laugh less	7. Laugh more
8. Be more rational	8. Be less rational
9. Be more serious	9. Be less serious
10. Stay home more	10. Go out more
11. Change less	11. Change more
12. Pay less attention to clothes	12. Pay more attention to clothes
13. Be less sensitive	13. Be more sensitive
14. Pay more attention to time	14. Pay less attention to time

2. How to handle our Differences

    a. _____ **them.** Ephesians 4:1-3 -- *I urge you to live a life worthy of the calling you have received. Be completely humble and gentle; be patient, **bearing with** one another in love. Make **every effort** to keep the unity of the Spirit through the bond of **peace**.*

CHAPTER 5 — CONSTRUCTIVE CONFLICT

Colossians 3:12-14 -- *Therefore, as God's chosen people, holy and dearly loved, clothe yourselves with compassion, kindness, humility, gentleness and patience.* **Bear with** *each other and forgive whatever grievances you may have against one another. Forgive as the Lord forgave you.*

Forbear...a forgotten word in our culture. Society says, "Don't put up with anybody!" But God says, "Put up with each other compassionately." Actually, "forbear" or "bear with" means more than simply "putting up" with someone. The Greek word literally means "to hold up." Therefore, to forbear is "to endure with gentleness, clemency, and a sweet reasonableness." (Vine's Expository Dictionary of New Testament Words)

b. See our partners' unique characteristics as _____ instead of _____.
1 Thessalonians 5:11 -- *Therefore encourage one another and build each other up....*
Romans 12:10 -- *Be devoted to one another in brotherly love. Honor one another above yourselves.* We tend to think, "**My** characteristics are **strengths**. So my partner's characteristics -- the ones different from mine -- **must be weaknesses**." It's hard for us to comprehend that our differences **are** our strengths. We need to abide in these two Scriptures, so that we will **build up** our mates and **honor their differences** as strengths.

CHAPTER 5 — CONSTRUCTIVE CONFLICT

   c. **Do not try to _____ our partners to be like ourselves.** Ephesians 5:1-2a -- *Be imitators of God, therefore, as dearly loved children and live a life of love....* The plan is -- we **both** imitate God. He never suggests we should expect our mates to imitate us. Our mates can't possibly imitate God and us at the same time anyway!

B. Power Struggles

1. What are Power Struggles?

_____ = the ability of one spouse to influence or control the other.

_____ = the battle for power.

James, the brother of our Lord Jesus, was right when he said, *What causes fights and quarrels*

CHAPTER 5   CONSTRUCTIVE CONFLICT

among you? Don't they come from your desires that battle within you? You want something but don't get it.... (James 4:1-2a). How aptly that describes power struggles: we *want something but don't get it.* We'd be far better off to believe the truth. And that is: we are not in **competition** with one another; we are **interdependent** with one another. We are not two fists, fighting for control. We are **one** fist made of **two hands, fingers interlocked**.

2. Ways to _____ the power of Power Struggles.

   a. _____ **what you have been doing does not work.** This is absolutely necessary. If you believe your struggle for power has been successful, you probably won't abandon it.

   b. _____ **your mind enough to see your spouse's point of view.** In the power struggle role-play, the wife could have said to herself (apply a little Thot-Talk here), "It seems like the more I bug him about this, the more he backs away. He must be backing off for a reason. What is it?" And the husband could say to himself (more Thot-Talk), "She keeps telling me she wants me to talk to her instead of watching TV. Hmm, maybe she really **does** need my attention."

   c. _____ **your hold on your own point of view.** Just because your point of view is **right** does not mean your partner's is **wrong**. You might be fighting a battle that doesn't need to be fought. Both spouses could continue their Thot-Talk, "Perhaps I'm not seeing this whole thing in perspective. I guess my point of view isn't the only one to consider here."

d. _____ **your mate what he/she really wants in a situation.** The husband could say, "Sweetheart, you keep handing me that 'honey-do' list of yours. Do you want me to get that list done, or do you resent my watching TV, or what? Tell me what you really want me to do." The wife could say, "Honey, I feel like you don't want to spend time with me and our kids anymore. Can I ever approach you about my needs? Or is it only when you're watching TV that you don't want to hear about them? Tell me what you really want me to do." What a simple statement, "Tell me what you want me to do." When said in a **quiet, loving** way, it works miracles. And after your mate awakens from a dead faint, you can move on to the next step.

e. _____ **your mate the freedom to choose whether he/she will abide by your request.** (that's *request* not *demand*). You might be asking the impossible of your mate. Or he/she might be feeling too stubborn at the moment to acquiesce. Either way, the choice is your spouse's, not yours. Are you willing to **not** get your way about this? Perhaps it's time to read James 4 again and take a motive check.

f. _____ **what you are going to do.** You've given your mate a choice about your request; now it's time to choose whether **you** will abide by **your mate's** request. Before you decide, consider Romans 12:18 -- *If it is possible, as far as it **depends on you**, live at peace with everyone* [even your mate].

CHAPTER 5 — CONSTRUCTIVE CONFLICT

C. Faulty Communication

The third cause of conflict is our faulty communication patterns. What do we mean by this? Don't we talk right? Well, maybe not. Let's look at six patterns of communication that fuel the fires of conflict. In a sense, these are six ways we don't talk -- or listen -- right.

1. _____. This is a habit...a bad habit. When we practice habits over a long period of time, they wear ruts into our lives. We'll call this one the **"gripe rut."** A "gripe rut" is full of criticism, complaints, whining, and accusations. Some of us grew up in homes where the deep rut of criticism tripped everyone in the family. It was an uncomfortable rut and we hated it. Yet we perpetuate it. Why? Because it is a habit. But habits can be **broken** -- with work.

   Ephesians 4:29-32 -- *Do not let **any unwholesome talk** come out of your mouth, but only what is helpful for **building others up**...Get rid of...every form of malice. Be kind and compassionate to one another....*

2. **Avoiding talking about concerns for fear of _____.** When one partner fears conflict, he or she often avoids talking about any matter of concern or frustration. Their motive is to keep the peace by **avoiding the issues**. They don't want to "rock the boat." But as unresolved issues pile up, a storm of resentment begins to brew inside that spouse. And resentment, if not handled correctly, can produce **indifference**. Sooner or later, the one who avoids conflict at any cost may no longer **care** about the relationship at all.
   (Ephesians 4:25) *...put off falsehood and speak truthfully...for we are all members of one body.*

CHAPTER 5   CONSTRUCTIVE CONFLICT

3. **Talk-talk-talking instead of _____.**
We have the crazy idea the more we talk to our mates about a particular concern or situation, the more we will influence them to do what we want. The truth is -- the **more** we talk, the **less** our mates listen. When we verbally overload them, they tune us out. Someone has said: women are prone to **nag**, and men are prone to **badger**. Both nagging and badgering come down to the same thing, don't they? -- Talking instead of listening. Solomon said it was like Chinese water torture (Proverbs 19:13, liberally paraphrased). We need to practice what James 1:19 exhorts, *Everyone should be quick to listen, slow to speak....* In other words, we need to put a sock in it!

4. **Speaking in a _____ language --yours -- instead of your mate's.** Remember, one difference which causes conflict is being from different families of origin? This difference is seldom more conspicuous than in our communication patterns. Because we were reared with different values, beliefs and customs, we can use the same words but interpret them in entirely different ways. In some aspects, we talk to each other in a foreign language. We must study our mate as we would Latin or Greek. We need to concentrate on understanding that **deep person** we've promised to love, honor and cherish. This is one reason God intends marriage to be for life. We need our whole life time to discover the intricate person to whom we are married.

5. **Expressing yourself in _____ terms instead of _____.** When someone asked a man what his favorite wine was, he replied, "Why don't you ever listen to me?" (Wine -- whine?) Many of us have developed the habit of

expressing ourselves negatively. We say things like, "You don't have time to talk with me right now, do you?" Or, "Why don't you ever...?" Each of our negative whines can be rephrased in a positive way. Instead of, "You don't have time to talk with me right now, do you?" you can say, "I would really like to talk with you right now. Do you have time?" "Why don't you ever listen to me?" can become, "I have something important to tell you. I would really like you to listen to me for a moment."

6. Using _____ as a weapon. Norm Wright states more marriages today are dying from silence than from violence (<u>Making Peace With Your Partner</u>). We would have to agree with him. Silence is extremely **flammable** and feeds the fires of conflict.

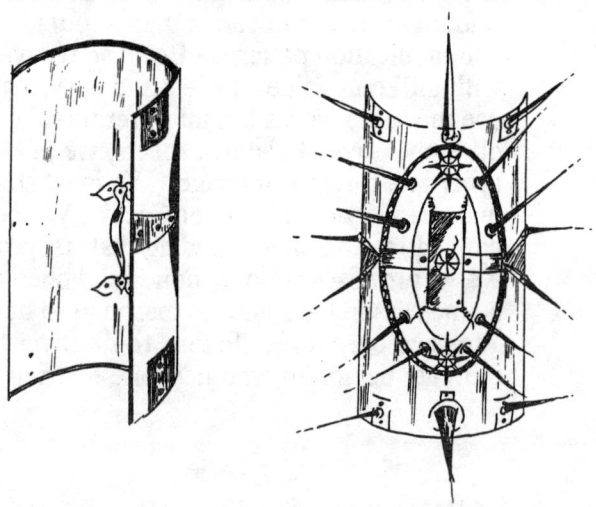

Ephesians 4:32. *Be kind and compassionate to one another....*

CHAPTER 5   CONSTRUCTIVE CONFLICT

IV. HOW TO HANDLE CONFLICT

Conflict can be as simple as a difference of opinion, but when it erupts into anger, we need to know what to do. Let's look at how to handle it from both sides: first from the viewpoint of the one receiving the anger, and then from the viewpoint of the one who is angry.

A. What to do when your _____ is angry and ready for conflict.

    1. Give your partner _____ to be angry with you. This is probably the most important step we can take to accept our mates when they are angry. By reminding ourselves it is **all right** for them to be angry, we not only accept our partners in their anger, we also accept the **fact** they **are** angry. When we see anger kicking open our mates' emotional doors, we need to practice positive Thot-Talk such as, "It is O.K. for my mate to be angry. He/she isn't a horrible person just because he's angry." You'd be surprised how much of the conflict this will diffuse, because it helps keep us from jumping into the fray.

CHAPTER 5   CONSTRUCTIVE CONFLICT

Philippians 2:4 reminds us that our mate's concerns (even if they are shrouded in anger) are worthy of our interest: *Each of you should look not only to your own interests, but also to the interests of others.*

2. **Don't _____ your spouse for becoming angry with you.** That is, don't jump right into battle with your dukes up. This may sound crazy, but that in itself somehow rewards your mate for expressing anger. Instead, say something like, "I can understand your being angry and upset." That sentence alone may stop the whole confrontation, for when your mates regains consciousness, they may not remember they were even angry. Ecclesiastes 7:9 is wise counsel: *Do not be **quickly provoked** in your spirit, for anger resides in the lap of fools.*

3. **Ask your partner to speak in a _____ manner.** It's O.K. to respond to your partners' yelling in a calm and neutral way, such as, "Would you please restate that in a lower voice so I can better understand you?" Your spouse has the right to be angry, but not the right to yell. The key words here are **calm** and **neutral**. We could also add: **nonjudgmental**. A gentle and nonjudgmental answer at this time will go a long way in calming your spouse's anger. Proverbs 15:1-- *A gentle answer turns away wrath.*

4. **_____ _____ _____ just because your mate is angry.** Are you thinking, "I'm not made of stone. I can't do that!"? We encourage you to give it a try. If you decide now, while you are **calm**, **not to respond in anger** the next time your spouse is angry, you just might surprise yourself. You may be stronger than you

CHAPTER 5   CONSTRUCTIVE CONFLICT

think. God knows you are capable of pulling this off with His help, or He wouldn't have said things like Proverbs 12:16 -- *A fool shows his annoyance at once, but a prudent man overlooks an insult,* and James 1:19 -- *Everyone should be quick to listen, slow to speak and slow to become angry.*

5. **Identify your _____ that contributes to the conflict.** Analyze your conflicts. Is there a **pattern** to them? Do you say or do the same kind of things over and over again; things that seem to push your partner's buttons? Focus only on **your** actions. Don't allow yourself to start throwing blame at your mate. The goal is for you to discover **your part** in the conflicts. If you think conflict is a serious problem in your marriage, keep a notebook of your fights to help analyze the problem. Record what you say and do, and what your partner says and does. You might even need to tape record one or two of your arguments to analyze later when you are calm.

It's important that you concentrate on **your contribution** to the fight, **not your mate's**. It's your mate's job to analyze his/her own contribution -- not yours. This sounds like a lot of work, doesn't it? But if you are really serious about finding **solutions** to your conflict, this could be a very important step. Remember, God promises to give you understanding if you are teachable. Proverbs 15:32b -- *...whoever heeds correction gains understanding.*

B. **What to do when _____ are angry and ready for conflict.**

    1. **_____.** The old saying about "counting to ten" is not as trite as you might think. When you feel anger rising up inside you, put on the brakes,

wait a little and think about how you should handle it. Listen to Nehemiah's wise counsel: *I was very angry when I heard their cry and these words. I thought it over, **then** rebuked the nobles and officials....* (Nehemiah 5:6-7, Amplified Version).

2. **Express your anger in a _____ way.** You can say something like, "I'm getting angry," or "I'm losing control." When you make a neutral statement like that, you are not issuing a challenge to fight. You are being honest and acknowledging your feelings. This step is imperative if you are going to handle your anger effectively. It isn't easy. You will have to guard your emotions and keep them under control. You will also have to keep your **mouth** under control. Proverbs 21:23 -- *He who guards his mouth and his tongue keeps himself from calamity.*

3. **_____ yourself to not yell or raise your voice.** This is another commitment you must make while you are **calm**. It's best to talk about it as a couple, and make a **mutual commitment** to not raise your voices or lose self-control during a fight. However, if one or both of you begins to spin out of control during a conflict, the best course of action is to **stop** the fight until after you both have calmed down. This is called *suspending the anger*. Proverbs 17:27 reminds us of the importance of such discipline: *A man of knowledge uses words with **restraint**, and a man of understanding is even-tempered.*

It is important to keep in mind you are not moving away from the issue forever. You must resolve it in a timely manner, because you don't want to

CHAPTER 5   CONSTRUCTIVE CONFLICT

bury it alive. Issues buried alive grow stronger under ground and have the annoying habit of resurrecting at the most inconvenient times.

4. _____ your anger.

You don't want to be angry, but you are. Instead of a declaration of war, you have issued an invitation to negotiate. Proverbs 20:3a declares this is the honorable thing to do: *It is to a man's honor to avoid strife....*

5. **Ask your partner for _____.** This might be hard on your pride, but it will certainly make things easier on your relationship. The issue of conflict becomes a problem for the two of you to solve, rather than a wall of alienation to separate you.

You can take this one step further by giving your partner **permission** to let you know when he/she sees you becoming angry. (See Chapter 3 for more details.) It is essential to humbly acknowledge your need for help in this area. Proverbs 19:20 -- *Listen to advice and accept instruction, and in the end you will be wise.*

6. **After the conflict, do some _____ -- Review and Rehearse.**

   a. **Review** -- After you both have **cooled down**, do some discovery together about the conflict. This is not for the purpose of placing blame, but simply to find out what **triggered** it. Was the conflict part of a pattern? What contributed to your feelings of anger? What emotion was hidden under your anger? This is review.

CHAPTER 5 — CONSTRUCTIVE CONFLICT

b. Rehearse -- Talk about what you could do differently when a similar situation occurs. Suggest things to do to make the situation less volatile. This is especially helpful for **patterns** of conflict. If you fight about the same things over and over again, you must start doing something **different**, or that pattern will develop into a very thick wall.

Proverbs 19:8 -- *He who gets wisdom loves his own soul; he who cherishes understanding prospers.*

V. GOD'S PROMISE -- OUR COOPERATION.

A. God's ladder of promise:

                _____
                (Prov. 29:11b)
                And will help you keep yourself under control.

            _____
            (Prov. 19:11b)
            It will make you able to overlook offenses

        _____ (Prov. 19:11a)
      And wisdom, in turn, will give you patience

    _____ (Prov. 19:20b)
That will make you wise.

_____ (Prov. 19:20a)
Listen to advice and accept instruction

B. God's formula for _____:

Ephesians 4:32 -- *Be **kind** and **compassionate** to one another, **forgiving** each other, just as in Christ God forgave you.* We promised you this verse, remember? It begins by imploring us to be kind and compassionate to one another. If we really had this attitude, most of our fights would never happen, would they? **Kindness -- compassion** -- such simple words. But we see so little of them in conflictive relationships. In fact, their absence is a distinctive trait of couples who have a lot of conflict. Oh, how **we all need** kindness and compassion! And oh, how our mates need **our** kindness and compassion!

The second appeal in verse 32 is that we **forgive** like God forgives us. We've talked about forgiveness several times already...and we'll talk about it more before we're finished. **Forgiveness** is one of the most important subjects in Scripture. There are at least one-hundred-and-twelve verses that talk about it (we counted). It's profoundly important to God, and profoundly important to us. **We can't live without it**--now or eternally. We need God's forgiveness; we need each other's. And we need to forgive as God forgives -- **unconditionally**.

VI. Conclusion

We can not afford for our Holy Wedlock to become Holy Deadlock. Unless we determine to do something about the way we handle conflict, we may find ourselves alone, on opposite sides of a wall neither of us can climb over. We don't want the German poet Gerta's words to be true of us: *Every time I hear the wedding march, I think of soldiers going off to war.* We want the **Holy Spirit's words** to describe our marriage: *Peacemakers who sow in peace raise a harvest of righteousness* (James 3:18).

CHAPTER 5   CONSTRUCTIVE CONFLICT

VII. GROUP DISCUSSION QUESTIONS:

1. What advice would you give to Mike and Joanie?

2. Which of the five DIFFERENCES do you think cause the most conflict? How?

3. Of the six faulty communication patterns, which do you tend to practice?

4. Of the five suggestions for handling your spouse's anger, which do you feel would be the most difficult to apply? Why?

5. Of the six suggestions for handling your anger, which one will you need the most help applying? Why

VIII. COUPLE SHARING:

1. I feel our greatest difference is _____. Of the 3 suggestions for handling differences, the one I need to apply the most is _____.

2. Our power struggles seem to center around

   _____

   _____ (if unable to identify a specific area, then acknowledge to one another that YOU DO engage in power struggles). Of the three suggestions for breaking the vicious cycle, this is the one I most need to apply:

   _____.

3. When you (speaking to your mate) are angry with me, the suggestion I will try hardest to apply is

   _____

4. When I am angry with you, the suggestion I will try hardest to apply is _____

   _____

So they are no longer two, but one. (Matt.19:6)

GOOD DECISIONS ARE COUPLE DECISIONS

I. INTRODUCTION

Couples often behave like they are room mates instead of a team. They make decisions that affect each other or their relationship without even consulting their partners. The key word -- *partners*. We could never get away with making solitary decisions in a business partnership. What makes us think it's good, sound policy for our marriage partnership? First of all, let's discuss **why** we should make decisions together.

II. WHY MAKE DECISIONS TOGETHER?

A. Because we are _____.

1. They shall leave father and mother and be _____.

Genesis 2:23-24 -- *The man said, "This is now bone of my bones and flesh of my flesh; she shall be called 'woman,' for she was taken out of man." For this reason a man will leave his father and mother and be united to his wife, and they will become one flesh.*

2. The uniqueness of the marriage relationship emphasized by _____.

Matthew 19:4-6 -- *"Haven't you read," He replied, "that at the beginning the Creator 'made them male and female,' and said, 'For this reason a man will leave his father and mother and be united to his wife, and the two will become one flesh'? So they are no longer two, but one. Therefore what God has joined together, let man not separate."* Jesus refers to the same mystery of the marriage relationship (one - two - one), and adds, *So they are no longer two, but **one***. God looks at us as a married couple and sees **One Unit**.

3. The uniqueness of the marriage relationship reiterated by _____.

Ephesians 5:31-32 -- *"For this reason a man will leave his father and mother and be united to his wife, and the two will become one flesh." This is a profound mystery -- but I am talking about Christ and the church.*

4. Our oneness is also like the oneness of the _____.

Deuteronomy 6:4--*Hear, O Israel: The Lord our God, the Lord is one.* The Hebrew word here for *one* is the same word used in Genesis. We as a married couple are **one**; the triune God is **one**. Can you grasp that? Our husband-wife oneness is like the relationship shared by the Trinity. No wonder Paul calls it a **profound mystery**.

CHAPTER 6   COUPLE DECISION-MAKING

B. Because it is _____.

> Proverbs 11:14 -- *For lack of guidance a nation falls, but many advisers make victory sure.* 13:10 -- *Pride only breeds quarrels, but wisdom is found in those who take advice.* 15:22 -- *Plans fail for lack of counsel, but with many advisers they succeed.* Get the picture? **It's too risky to make decisions on your own.** It's safer to have counsel from others. And the very best counselor you could ever have...specially made for you...uniquely qualified...is your mate.

C. Because we both need to _____ the decision and the _____.

> If you **both** don't own the decision, can you **both** own the results? Is it fair for you to expect your mate to live with the results -- sometimes disastrous results -- of **your** decisions?

CHAPTER 6   COUPLE DECISION-MAKING

III. WHAT MAKING COUPLE DECISIONS DOES _____ MEAN:

A. That each spouse loses his/her individual _____.

We are **one**, but we are still **two**. Like the personalities of the Godhead, we can, at the same time, be **two persons forming one unit**.

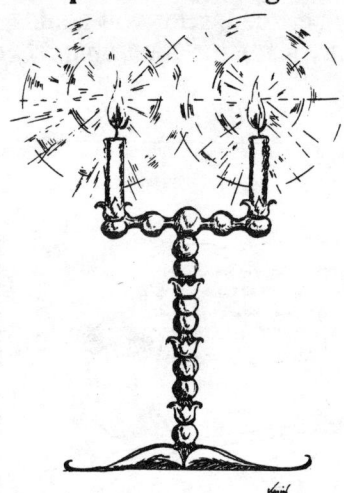

B. That both spouses _____ alike.

We know you can't possibly think alike about everything. And that's good, because you shouldn't if you are going to make good couple decisions. No, you don't have to think **alike**, but you do have to **think**; and you need to **share** what you're thinking with each other.

C. That there will never be _____.

Uh-oh, did we shock you? Because you do not think exactly alike, you might experience some conflict along the way to making good decisions together. We never said making couple decisions was **easy**; we just said it was **best**.

CHAPTER 6   COUPLE DECISION-MAKING

D. That decisions which do not _____ _____ must be made by both spouses.

If a decision doesn't affect you as a couple or as a family, then, by all means, make it yourself.

IV. WHAT COUPLE DECISION MAKING _____ MEAN.

A. That both spouses talk over _____ decisions that affect both _____ either makes up his/her own mind about the matter.

How many times do we come together to discuss a decision, already knowing what **we** want? Our goal for the discussion is actually to talk our partners into seeing things **our** way. Be honest, now. Isn't that your agenda sometimes?

B. That both spouses discuss and agree on decisions that affect both before _____ others or _____ on a decision.

When someone wants your answer on a decision that should be made by both of you, don't be embarrassed to say simply, "Since that affects my spouse too, I'll talk it over with him/her and get back with you." Even if you're given a great opportunity to invest money in the deal of a life time, wait and talk it over with your mate. It's his/her money too. Or if a friend asks you to dinner, tell them you'll check with your mate and call them back.

C. That a satisfactory solution is reached that can be _____ by both.

Owning the **decision** and **results** is not just a reason for making decisions together, it is an absolute necessity. We must take **ownership** of our decisions. If we don't, we will live a life of resentment and blame.

D. That the goal becomes _____ _____ and our _____ _____.

The **first** question a couple should ask when trying to make a decision is, "What would **God** have us do?" The **second** question they should ask is, "Will this **increase** our oneness or **decrease** it?" So often, we approach decisions without giving God or our coupleness a second thought. But if we are to make good couple decisions, we need to recognize that **God's will** and **our coupleness** are the two **most important considerations**.

Proverbs 3:5-6 are such well known verses, we quote them without even thinking how profound they are. They can change forever the way we approach decisions. *Trust in the Lord with all your heart and lean not on your own understanding; in all your ways acknowledge him, and he will make your paths straight [will direct your paths].*

V. SUBMISSION -- HEADSHIP

A. The Big Picture for wives:

Submission, what a word! We've seen people react to it like angry dogs and like limp doormats. What does the Bible really teach about it? Who's suppose to be submissive? And what does it have to do with making decisions?

1. What does the Bible teach?

1 Peter chapters 2 and 3 teach specifically about submission. In 2:9 and following, the Apostle Peter labels us a chosen people, a called people...called to live like Jesus...called to live a life of submission. Throughout the rest of chapter 2 and most of chapter 3, Peter paints pictures of what "called people" look like in different walks of life.

In verses 21-25, Peter focuses our attention on Jesus Christ, and explains **why** we are called to a life of submission: *because Christ suffered for you, leaving you an example, that you should follow in his steps.* What is the example Jesus left us? *...No deceit was found in his mouth....When they hurled their insults at him, he did not retaliate; when he suffered, he made no threats. Instead, he entrusted himself to him who judges justly [the Father].* This is the example we are to follow...the steps of Jesus...the steps of submission.

Now we come to chapter 3. This is not a separate teaching but a continuation of what Peter started in chapter 2, that is, Christians are called to a life of submission. Verse 1 begins with *Wives, **in the same way** be submissive to your husbands.* In what "same way" is Peter talking about? The way Jesus exemplified. The way Christian citizens and employees are commanded to live. We, as wives, like Sarah of old, are called to a life of submission. We are called to walk in the steps of Jesus.

2. Who is supposed to be submissive?

Peter wants to make absolutely sure he doesn't leave anyone out, so he continues in verses 8 and 9 with, *Finally, **all of you**, live in harmony with one another; be sympathetic, love as brothers, be compassionate and humble. Do not repay evil with evil or insult with insult, but with blessing, because to this you were called so that you may inherit a blessing.* Do these verses remind you of the description of Jesus in chapter 2? Did you notice the words *to this you were called?* **As Christians, no matter who we are or what we do, we are called to a life of submission...just**

like Jesus.
Submission simply means *to defer or yield to the wishes of another.* It's basically a military term, referring to rank or job position. There's no thought in it of one person being better or smarter than another. Submission is simply a **non-rebellious attitude** of life.

B. The Big Picture for husbands:

We've already looked at the reference to husbands in 1 Peter 3. But we don't want them to feel slighted, so let's talk more specifically about headship.

1. What does the Bible teach?

The apostle Paul echoes Peter's theme of submission in Ephesians 5 and 6. Verses 22 and 23 state, *Wives, submit to your husbands as to the Lord. For the husband is head of the wife as Christ is the head of the church....* We've heard these verses misused to prove that husbands are **kings** and wives their **subjects**. But let's look more closely, because this Scripture teaches something completely different from that.

First of all, this section of Ephesians 5 actually begins with often-overlooked verse 21: ***Submit to one another** out of reverence for Christ.* Paul, like Peter, then describes what submission looks like in different walks of life. He mentions wives, husbands, children, fathers, slaves and masters.

We husbands especially cherish verse 23, though we usually only memorize the first phrase: *the husband is the head of the wife....* When I

(Harold) was a young man, I took this verse and ran with it. Bette was to submit to me, because I was the head! I wasn't quite sure what a head was supposed to be, but **I was it**. One day, I finally looked at the rest of the verse, *For the husband is the head of the wife as Christ is the head of the church, his body, of which he is the Savior.* I decided if I am supposed to be *the head* **like Christ**, then I'd better find out what kind of *head* Christ is. The rest of this passage gave me some clues. Verse 25 urged me to love my wife sacrificially like Christ loves the church. Verse 28 commanded me to love her like I love my own body. And verse 33 said I must love her like I love myself.

Searching further, I found that Philippians 2:5-11 presented an even clearer picture of the kind of *head* Christ is, and therefore, the kind of *head* I am to be: *Your attitude should be the same as that of Christ Jesus: Who, being in very nature God, did not consider equality with God something to be grasped, but made himself nothing, taking the very nature of a servant, being made in human likeness. And being found in appearance as a man, he humbled himself and became obedient to death -- even death on a cross....* That doesn't sound like a **dictator** to me. Christ was a **servant-leader** whose strength was displayed in **humility**.

2. What does this mean?

A servant-leader leads by example (1 Peter 2:21). So, husbands, if we want to be the right kind of *heads*, then we must learn to be **servant-leaders** like Jesus Christ.

Husbands and wives, we have been called to **mutual submission** to the Lord and to one another. **We have both been called to be like Jesus.**

CHAPTER 6   COUPLE DECISION-MAKING

C. What does this have to do with decision making?

The only way for God to direct us into His will is for us to **submit** ourselves to Him. It follows then, that when we make decisions as a couple, we must come to Him in **mutual submission**. Here are some **guidelines** to follow in making couple decisions the right way.

1. _____ together for God's direction, submitting your wills to Him. Philippians 4:6 -- *Do not be anxious about anything, but in everything, by prayer and petition, with thanksgiving, **present your requests to God.***

2. _____ your rights. If you approach a decision while demanding your own rights, you essentially jam the process. Philippians 2:3 -- *Do nothing out of **selfish ambition or vain conceit**, but in humility consider others better than yourselves.*

3. Maintain an attitude of _____: to God and to one another. James 4:7a -- ***Submit yourselves, then, to God.*** Ephesians 5:21 -- ***Submit to one another out of reverence for Christ.***

4. _____ God's Word for direction. If the Bible says something definitive about your specific decision or plans, obey that directive. Psalm 119:105 -- ***Your Word is a lamp to my feet and a light for my path.***

5. _____ a pro and con list.

Luke 14:28 -- *Suppose one of you wants to build a tower. Will he not first **sit down and estimate the cost** to see if he has enough money to complete it?* We are urged to "sit down and estimate" before we decide.

6. If you still can't reach a decision, _____ a godly friend (someone you respect) to help you discover together all the options open to you. Proverbs 19:20 -- ***Listen to advice** and accept instruction, and in the end you will be wise.*

7. _____ for God's answer.

Proverbs 19:2 -- *It is not good to have zeal without knowledge, nor to be **hasty** and miss the way.* Psalm 37:34a -- ***Wait for the Lord** and keep his way.*

Something wonderful happens in us and in our marriages when we stop digging in our heels and fighting to get our own way...when we **stop** acting like two independent individuals living together and **start** acting like a team. **We are a team. Jesus Himself calls us a team.** Matthew 19:6 -- *So they are no longer two, but one.* **Let's start acting like it!**

CHAPTER 6　　　　　　COUPLE DECISION-MAKING

VI. GROUP DISCUSSION QUESTIONS

1. Case Study #1

Pretend this couple is coming to you for advice: A Christian husband and wife have lived in the same town for 10 years and are very active in their church. The husband has a fine position with a good company, but he does not like his work. He has been offered another position -- 3,000 miles away, in a colder climate and at less pay. He wants to accept the position because it is the type of work he has always wanted to do. He talks with his wife and tells her he is thinking of taking the job. She does not want him to accept it and gives her reasons. She says she definitely won't move. What would you advise them to do?

2. Case Study #2

Here is another couple coming to ask for your wise counsel: A Christian couple has been very active in an evangelical church. For some time, though, the husband has been interested in the Mormon church and finally decides to join that church and becomes a Mormon. His wife does not know what to do. The Scriptures say to submit, but does that mean she should follow her husband, leave her church and take the children with her to the Mormon church? What would you advise her to do? How would you advise the husband?

3. From your observation of other couples and your own experience, list some common decision-making practices among couples that ought to change. How would the principles we've learned make a difference in them?

CHAPTER 6   COUPLE DECISION-MAKING

VII. COUPLE SHARING QUESTIONS

1. How do I feel about the way we now make decisions? According to the principles we have heard, I would like to start (list at least one new practice from the decision-making guidelines): _____

   _____.

2. Were some of **our** decision-making practices mentioned in the group discussion session? Which ones? How can we change them?

3. Hold hands and pray together (if you can not pray out loud, pray silently): "Lord, we want to be more like you. You showed us how to be servants. We want to be your servants and servants to one another. Help us learn to be mutually submissive--to you, Lord, and to one another. And help us make decisions Your way. In Jesus name, Amen."

I am my beloved's, and my beloved is mine.... (Song of Sol. 6:3 KJV)

ROMANCE & SEX

I. INTRODUCTION--

A. Sexual liberation movement

1. **In the last two or three decades there has been a drastic change in the public acceptance of the subject of sex.** There are sexual connotations in display ads on billboards, newspapers, magazines, television -- it's almost impossible NOT to be confronted by a scantily clothed, beautiful-to-look-at female or buff male on a daily basis from one source or another.

2. **This movement has failed dismally in the most important part of sexuality:** keeping romance and commitment part of the sexual experience. "Shacking up" together for a time or having one night flings with no "ties" or even romance, has become common.

B. The love people yearn for includes _____.

1. **The following is a quote from an Ann Landers'** survey in FAMILY CIRCLE on June 11, 1985:

   <u>*After tabulating 90,000 responses, we published the results. The verdict was clear: A solid 72%*</u>

> *of the women said "Yes," they would be content to be held close and treated tenderly and forget about the act. Of those 72%, 40% were under 40 years of age.*

What does this say to us men? It should at least shock us into a little romancing and make us open our ears to the rest of this session! Marriages are dying for lack of romance. We all need to invest ourselves in being more romantic.

2. **Romance is not foreign to the Bible.** Have you read the Book of Ruth? Pretty romantic. Proverbs is full of insights into romance. And, of course, the Song of Solomon is devoted solely to marital romantic love. In fact, marital romance and love must be a very important subject to our Father. He dedicated an entire book in His Word to it. Can you think of any other subject besides salvation that He does that for?

C. This type of love -- love that includes romance and commitment -- demands that we grow in _____. **Listen to the kind of love God wants for our marriages.**

1 Corinthians 13:4-7 -- *Love is patient, love is kind. It does not envy, it does not boast, it is not proud. It is not rude, it is not self-seeking, it is not easily angered, it keeps no record of wrongs. Love does not delight in evil but rejoices with the truth. It always protects, always trusts, always hopes, always perseveres.*

If you practice this kind of love, you can be sure of intimacy in your marriage relationship. There are different kinds of intimacies. We're going to mention just four. And remember, we need to grow in each of these.

CHAPTER 7 — ROMANCE & SEX

1. Emotional Intimacy.

"Walls"

Their wedding picture mocked them from the table, these two
whose minds no longer touched each other.

They lived with such a heavy barricade between them that
neither battering ram of words nor artilleries of touch
could break it down.

Somewhere, between the oldest child's first tooth and the
youngest daughter's graduation, they lost each other

Throughout the years, each slowly unraveled that tangled ball
of string called self, and as they tugged at stubborn
knots each hid his searching from the other.

Sometimes she cried at night and begged the whispering darkness
to tell her who she was.

He lay beside her, snoring like a hibernating bear, unaware
of her winter.

Once, after they had made love, he wanted to tell her how
afraid he was of dying, but fearing to show his naked
soul, he spoke instead about the beauty of her breasts.

She took a course in modern art, trying to find herself in
colors splashed upon a canvas, and complaining to
other
women about men who were insensitive.

> *He climbed a tomb called "the office," wrapped his mind in*
> *a shroud of paper figures and buried himself in customers.*
>
> *Slowly, the wall between them rose, cemented by the mortar*
> *of indifference.*
>
> *One day, reaching out to touch each other, they found a barrier*
> *they could not penetrate, and recoiling from the coldness*
> *of the stone, each retreated from the stranger on the*
> *other side.*
>
> *For when love dies, it is not in a moment of angry battle,*
> *nor when fiery bodies lose their heat.*
>
> *It lies panting, exhausted, expiring at the bottom of a wall*
> *it could not scale.*
>
> (Source unknown)

2. **Aesthetic Intimacy.** This is sharing the "we" experiences of our lives, like watching a sunset together, or your child's ballgame. It's taking a walk along the beach or sharing a special moment in time. But it doesn't even have to be a positive moment. It can be the agonizing times, such as clinging to one another, waiting for a doctor's diagnosis. It's creating history together, and it is powerful in the bonding process.

3. **Spiritual Intimacy.** This is the sharing together of our lives and faith in Christ. This intimacy, more than any other, breeds trust in our relationship as husband and wife. We'll be talking a lot more about this in chapter 11. So, hang in there.

CHAPTER 7 — ROMANCE & SEX

4. **Physical Intimacy.** Ah, this is what you've been waiting for. But you know what? Physical intimacy is the culmination of the other intimacies. For the two bodies that come together physically house two persons who should already be intimate.

II. THE ART OF ROMANCE

A. Why romance _____.

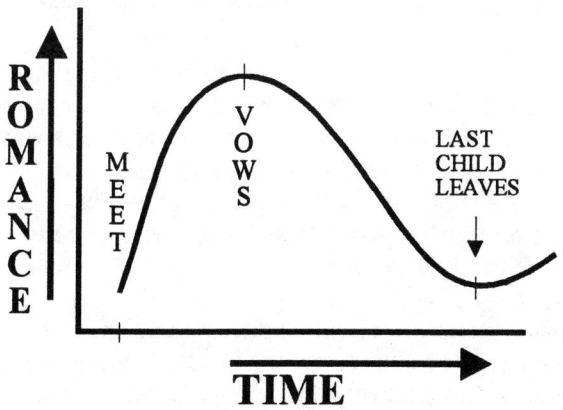

Romance naturally declines in such an atmosphere because romance demands that attention be placed on the other partner. Romance must be "other" centered. We can change the direction of our romance curve at any point we choose to **refocus our attention** on our mate's needs instead of our own. The romance curve can be altered at any point such a decision is made and carried through.

B. How to help our _____ make our marriages romantic.

CHAPTER 7 — ROMANCE & SEX

1. _____ **attitude** -- remember all that stuff about thot-talk? Go back and look at that chapter again, and apply it to the bedroom. No, on second thought, apply it all day long, and see the difference it will make in your bedroom.

   Philippians 4:8 instructs, *Finally, brothers, whatever is true, whatever is noble, whatever is right, whatever is pure, whatever is lovely, whatever is admirable--if anything is excellent or praiseworthy--think about such things.*

   Now, let's read that Scripture again, applying it to our marriages. *Finally, brothers and sisters, whatever is true **about your mate**, whatever is noble **about your mate**, whatever is right **about your mate**, whatever is pure **about your mate**, whatever is lovely **about your mate**, whatever is admirable **about your mate**--if anything is excellent or praiseworthy **about your mate**--think about such things.*

   Nothing kills romance faster than criticism. Nothing builds romance faster than the positive thot-talk commanded in this verse.

2. _____ **build strong romantic attitudes**. When is the last time you gave your mate a compliment? If you are sitting there thinking, "Yeah, but when's the last time he/she gave me one," then you need to redirect your focus off yourself onto your mate (remember why romance declines?).

CHAPTER 7   ROMANCE & SEX

3. _____ **helps build romance.** But you know this by now, don't you? There is nothing quite so romantic as sharing your hopes and dreams together. That's probably what stirred up the fires of romance between you two in the first place. Remember those long talks when you were courting?

4. _____ **-- doing those things that you know your mate enjoys and appreciates creates romantic feelings.** Taking her hand, catching his eye across the room, opening her door, wearing his favorite nightie are just a few examples.

CHAPTER 7   ROMANCE & SEX

C. Things we can _____ to make our marriages more romantic.

 1. **Recapture the mystery and excitement of earlier days.**

    a. **What was your dating like** in early marriage? Be that way again!

    b. **What experiences were special?** They were probably **planned** -- not **spontaneous**. Plan for "special times" now.

CHAPTER 7   ROMANCE & SEX

(1) **Good romantic relationships take _____**: Baby-sitting, scheduling, setting the mood with flowers, candlelight, clothing, music, perfume -- appeal to all 5 senses to please your mate.

(2) **Be _____ about your dates --**

On our 10th Anniversary, Bette thought I was simply taking her out to a nice dinner at a restaurant that overlooked the beach in Ventura, California. The baby-sitter that had been arranged was not one we would leave our kids with for an extended period of time. She didn't know I had arranged for a more mature woman to come in several hours later to stay the night while I whisked her off to a romantic getaway. I had arranged for a hotel room overlooking the Beach near the restaurant where we had reservations.

The suitcase was packed and in the trunk of the car. Packing her make-up and personal care stuff would have been a nightmare for me. Luckily her sister, Linda, dropped by that day. While Bette was involved with the kids, Linda excitedly helped me pack what she thought Bette would need out of all her paraphernalia. The only thing I forgot was her nightgown -- but that oversight worked out fine. (To this day she still thinks it was semi-intentional.)

After dinner we took a walk on the beach toward the pier. It happened to take us by "our" hotel. There Bette played right into my scheme as she mentioned she needed to find a restroom.

I replied that the hotel should have restrooms in their lobby, so we walked in. While Bette was otherwise occupied, I checked in at the Front Desk and picked up our room key.

When she came out, I was sitting innocently in the lobby waiting for her. As we started out to complete our walk, I complained about how far we would have to trudge back to the car once we got to the pier. I suggested that we get the car and park closer. She agreed, but when I drove the car into the hotel's parking lot (which was real close to the pier), she cried, "But the sign says they'll tow the car away if we park here! This lot is for hotel guests only."

I continued to park the car while I calmly pulled the key from my jacket and told her, "Well -- **we're** hotel guests, here's our room key. Let's go celebrate our 10th."

2. Spend _____ together regularly.

  a. Quality time. If the only time you give your mate is left-over time when you're too tired to think, much less communicate, then you are going to end up with a "left-over" relationship.

  b. Schedule it and keep it! Surely your marriage is as important as a business appointment or dental appointment. So schedule time together, and don't let anything usurp it!

  c. Alone. Sure, it's nice sometimes to be with other couples for fun, but make sure you take dates alone too. This is especially important if you have children. The best thing you can do for your children is ensure they have a Mommy and Daddy who love each other!

CHAPTER 7   **ROMANCE & SEX**

    d. Get away from the everyday -- the hum-drum. Get away from the phone, from interruptions and everyday stress.

    This is our prescription:

    1 X per week -- a date.
        It doesn't have to be fancy or expensive. Be creative.
    1 X per quarter -- an overnight.
    1 X per 6 months -- a weekend.

D. Romance is a part of making love. Men and women both need romancing. Each of us needs to feel like we are very special to our mates. So we both need to let our mates know how special they are to us. And don't forget, the romancing _____ when you wake up in the morning and _____. through the day. A popular book about marriage is entitled SEX BEGINS IN THE KITCHEN. Think about it.

III. SOME PRACTICAL DO'S OF MAKING LOVE

Hebrews 13:4 -- *Marriage should be honored by all, and the marriage bed kept pure, for God will judge the adulterer and all the sexually immoral.*

God says the marriage bed is "pure" or "undefiled," which means completely free from any contamination. The Holy Spirit, through the writer of Hebrews, uses this same word back in chapter 7 to describe Jesus Christ Himself. This means that according to God, the creator of sex, we can no more call marital intimacy dirty than we can call Jesus Christ dirty.

CHAPTER 7   ROMANCE & SEX

A. Be _____

    1. Never _____. We never have that right. It can do so much harm.

        a. The more aggressive spouse (the one with the greater sex drive) **can actually lower the more passive mate's sex drive by being too pursuing.**

        b. The partner who wants to try new things (oral sex, different positions, etc.) **must not demand these of the other one.**

        Guidelines:
        (1) Does the Bible say anything about it?
        (2) Is it loving?
        (3) Do we feel peace or guilt after we have finished?
        (4) Is it mutually agreed upon without pressure of any kind?
        (5) Are we being gentle with each other?

2. Do not _____ your mate into making him or her have sex because of guilt or fear or some negative emotion. That makes the memories of making-love negative and actually lowers the sex drive of the more passive spouse. Our memories of sex are extremely powerful. If the memories are good, the sex drive will improve.

B. Do not _____ once the fun begins.

1. Don't begin to talk about something _____. (i.e. "Did you remember to take the trash out?" "Oh, I forgot to put gas in the car today." "Did you air up that tire that was low when you were out with the car this afternoon?")

2. _____ on your mate. Focus on them. Show them how important they are to you by becoming engrossed with them and them alone.

C. Do not make _____ of one another.

To laugh at, or be unkind to, our partner at anytime can be devastating, but especially when they are at their most vulnerable. We are such fragile creatures. But never more fragile than when we are naked. Scripture says *Be kind to one another* (Ephesians 4:32) -- this applies to the bedroom as well as every other room in the house.

D. Give _____ and affirmation freely.
Giving compliments during love-making frees us to be better lovers because it takes our focus off our own inadequacies. Instead we focus our attention on our wife or husband and their pleasure. We can say things

like, "I really like to hold you." "I am so thankful for you." "Your body feels so good to me." "I like the way you do that." "I love touching you there."

E. Respect one another's need for _____
-- put a lock on the bedroom door. Now you "compartmentalized" mates may be thinking, "What in the world for? It's not a problem for me." While you "global" mates may be saying, "Right on!" And some of you may be saying, "Global, compartmentalized -- what are they talking about?"

Global -- all outside and internal events, happenings, emotions and thoughts are intermingled. The fight or harsh words in the morning are brought into the bedroom that night -- they can't be separated. For the global person, everything is in one "emotional drawer." One thing in the "drawer," even if it's stuck in the corner, affects everything else in the entire "drawer."

Compartmental -- each event, happening, emotion and thought can be segregated into separate areas or "compartments." The fight in the morning was a separate event from the lovemaking at night and so does not need to be confused or mixed together. For the compartmentalized person, everything is in a different "emotional drawer." You can pull out one, then shut it and pull out a different one. They are each neatly labeled and don't get mixed together.

F. Come _____ for the occasion -- or undressed. Wear what pleases each other -- sexy men's underwear, slinky nightgowns, whatever. Be clean and shaved (remember thoughtfulness).

G. **Make the _____ conducive to love-making.** Candles, soft music, a clean bedroom, perfume on the sheets -- all create a romantic atmosphere. Your bedroom is your special place; it should be the prettiest room in the house. Take a little trouble and time to make your intimate time together truly romantic. Both men and women crave romance. The SONG OF SOLOMON proves that. Read about some of the romantic places they made love!

H. **Pay _____** -- You are probably thinking, "Well, of course I pay attention!" But what we are talking about is active touching, or as the pros call it, sensate focus. Sensate focus is allowing yourself to be aware of the pleasure found in touch. It's giving yourself permission to admit that when your partner touches you in certain places, it feels good.

I. **Be _____** -- not the same way, the same place, the same time. Change the place, position, time, etc. -- Don't be afraid to try new things and new ways.

IV. CONCLUSION

God gave love-making to married couples as His gift of pleasure to be enjoyed to its fullest potential within the bonds of marriage. He designed it to be enjoyable to both the husband and the wife, and that enjoyment includes romance. Keep the Ann Landers' survey in mind as you continue to court each other. Get back into that **WIN** mode and **stay** there.

CHAPTER 7   ROMANCE & SEX

COUPLE SHARING OPTION #1
<u>SEXUAL INTIMACY DISCUSSION</u>

<u>Directions</u>: Complete the thoughts individually and alone, then share and discuss them with your spouse. If some of the questions are too intimidating, save them until later. But discuss as many as you can.

1. Before we were married, what I looked forward to most as I thought about our future sexual relationship was:

2. Before we were married, my greatest fantasy about you (or us) was:

3. In my mind, the best time(s) we have had sexually have been in (location):

4. To me, sex would be even more inviting if I:

5. To me, sex would be even more inviting if you:

6. The best time of day for me to "make love" is:

7. The worst time of the day for me to be sexually excited is:

8. At times when my sexual responses are slow, or I'm not in the mood, I'd generally like for you to:

CHAPTER 7　　　　　　　　　　　ROMANCE & SEX

9. The way (or words) I'd like to hear from you when you want to "make love" is (are):

10. When other people are around and you are thinking about "making love" let me know by:

11. When preparing for "making love," the most exciting things you can do for me are:

12. You turn me "on" the most when you:

13. I'd like you to touch me in the following ways when we "make love":

14. I'd like you to say the following things when we "make love":

15. With only positive growth in mind, the areas I believe we need to work on improving in our sexual relationship are:

ADDITIONAL COMMENTS:

CHAPTER 7 — ROMANCE & SEX

COUPLE SHARING OPTION #2

SENSATE FOCUS

This optional exercise should be fully agreed upon on a transparent level, otherwise it should be postponed until both spouses feel free to participate. This option is the experiencing of the "pleasuring". Make sure your room is comfortably warm and that you allow yourself the luxury of time (45 minutes minimum). Remember that continual feedback on the level of pleasure experienced is essential for your spouse to know what "pleasures" you the most. COMMUNICATE, COMMUNICATE, COMMUNICATE.

This exercise is primarily a communication exercise. Sex therapists often use it with couples having to agree beforehand that there will be no intercourse associated with the experience. Whether or not you allow that as an option is something you should discuss **prior** to entering into the exercise.

To begin, both partners need to disrobe to nudeness. One partner, either one, should lie face down on the bed while the other starts touching at the feet and slowly works his/her way up the back side of their partner's body. Continual feedback is desired as to the amount of "pleasure" the felt partner is receiving. We suggest a range of 1 to 10 with 10 being the greatest pleasure. The genitals are not to be included in this exercise -- we **know** that touch there brings pleasure.

The partner doing the touching should vary the touch from light to medium to heavy and should experiment with front of hands, back of hands and even cheeks and tongues for a variety of touch. Pay attention to the 6's and above -- these are areas that you should get back to later.

When the first partner has traversed the entire length of the body, then trade positions. If you cover the whole length of your partner's body in less than 10 minutes, you are going too fast! Slow down! When the process is complete for the second touching partner, then the one who started lying face down should again lie down, this time on his/her back.

The process again should proceed with the first touching partner starting at the feet and working his/her way to the top of the partner's head (don't be too quick in leaving the feet!). Again allow at least 10 or 15 minutes for this one process and get continual feedback concerning the amount of pleasure given. Once this portion is complete then again trade positions and have the second touching partner traverse from toe to head getting feedback all the while.

This whole four-part process should take around an hour to accomplish. If you cannot devote that much time to this option before one of you is zonked, then schedule this option for another time when you can.

CHAPTER 7 — ROMANCE & SEX

COUPLE SHARING OPTION #3

<u>Directions</u>: This is the Song of Solomon written in script form to be read together in private. The wife should read Shulamith's parts and the husband should read the King's parts. The other parts can be divided as desired.

The Most Beautiful Love Song Ever Written

Shulamith's First Days in the Palace (1:2-11)

The King's fiancee, Shulamith, in soliloquy

How I wish he would shower me with kisses for his exquisite kisses are more desirable than the finest wine. The gentle fragrance of your cologne brings the enchantment of springtime. Yes, it is the rich fragrance of your heart that awakens my love and respect. Yes, it is your character that brings you admiration from every girl of the court. How I long for you to come take me with you to run and laugh through the countryside of this kingdom. (You see, the King had brought me to the kingdom's palace.)

Women of the court to the King

We will always be very thankful and happy because of you, O King. For we love to speak of the inspiring beauty of your love.

Shulamith in soliloquy

They rightly love a person like you, my King.

Shulamith to women of the court

I realize that I do not display the fair and delicate skin of one raised in the comfort of a palace. I am darkened from the sun-- indeed, as dark as the tents of the humble desert nomads I used to work beside. But now I might say that I am also as dark as the luxurious drapery of the King's palace. Nevertheless, what loveliness I do have is not so weak that the gaze of the sun should make it bow its head in shame. And if the glare of the sun could not shame me, please know that neither will the glare of your contempt. I could not help it that my stepbrothers were angry with me and demanded that I work in the vineyard they had leased from the King. It was impossible for me to care for it and for the vineyard of my own appearance.

Shulamith to King

Please tell me, you whom I love so deeply, where you take your royal flock for its afternoon rest. I don't want to search randomly for you, wandering about like a woman of the streets.

Women of the court to Shulamith

If you do not know, O fairest among women, why not simply go ahead and follow the trail of the flocks, and then pasture your flock beside the shepherds' huts?

King to Shulamith

Your presence captivates attention as thoroughly as a single mare among a hundred stallions. And how perfectly your lovely jewelry and necklace adorn you lovely face.

Women of the court to Shulamith

We shall make even more elegant necklaces of gold and silver to adorn her face.

In a Palace Room (1:12-14)

Shulamith in soliloquy

While my King was dining at his table, my perfume refreshed me with its soothing fragrance. For my King is the fragrance and my thoughts of him are like a sachet of perfume hung around my neck, over my heart, continually refreshing me. How dear he is to me, as dear as the delicate henna blossoms in the oasis of En-Gedi. What joy I have found in that oasis!

In the Countryside (1:15-2:7)

King to Shulamith

You are so beautiful, my love. You are so beautiful. Your soft eyes are as gentle as doves.

Shulamith to King

And you are handsome, my love, and so enjoyable. It's so wonderful to walk through our home of nature together. Here

CHAPTER 7 — ROMANCE & SEX

the cool grass is a soft couch to lie upon, to catch our breath and to gaze at the beams and rafters of our house--the towering cedars and cypresses all around. Lying here I feel like a rose from the valley of Sharon, the loveliest flower in the valley.

King to Shulamith

Only the loveliest flower in the valley? No, my love. To me you are like a flower among thorns compared with any other woman in the world.

Shulamith to King

And you, my precious King, are like a fruitful apple tree among the barren trees of the forest compared with all the men in the world.

Shulamith in soliloquy

No longer do I labor in the heat of the sun. I find cool rest in the shade of this apple tree. Nourishment from its magical fruit brings me the radiant health only love brings. And he loves me so much. Even when he brings me to the great royal banquets attended by the most influential people in this kingdom and beyond, he is never so concerned for them that his love and his care for me is not as plain as a royal banner lifted high above my head.

How dear he is to me! My delightful peace in his love makes me so weak from joy that I must rest in his arms for strength. Yet such loving comfort makes me more joyful and weaker still. How I wish he could lay me down beside him and embrace me! But how important it is I promise, with the gentle gazelles and deer of the countryside as my witnesses, not to attempt to awaken love until love is pleased to awaken itself.

On the Way to the Countryside (2:8-17)

Shulamith in soliloquy

I hear my beloved. Look! He is coming to visit. And he is as dashing as a young stag leaping upon the mountains, springing upon the hills. There he is, standing at the door, trying to peer through the window and peep through the lattice. At last he speaks.

CHAPTER 7   ROMANCE & SEX

King to Shulamith

Come, my darling, my fair one, come with me. For look, the winter has passed. The rain is over and gone. The blossoms have appeared in the land. The time of singing has come, and the voice of the turtledove has been heard in the land. The fig tree has ripened its figs, and the vines in blossom have given forth fragrance. Let us go, my darling, my lovely one; come along with me. O my precious, gentle dove. You have been like a dove in the clefts of the mountain rocks, in the hidden places along the mountain trails. Now come out from the hidden place and let me see you. Let me hear the coo of your voice. For your voice is sweet and you are as gracefully beautiful as a dove in flight silhouetted against a soft blue sky. My love, what we have together is a valuable treasure; it is like a garden of the loveliest flowers in the world. Let us promise each other to catch any foxes that could spoil our garden when now at long last it blossoms for us.

Shulamith in soliloquy

My beloved belongs to me and I belong to him--this tender King who grazes his flock among the lilies.

Shulamith to King

How I long for the time when all through the night, until the day takes its first breath and the morning shadows flee from the sun, that you, my beloved King, might be a gazelle upon the hills of my breasts.

Shulamith Waits for Her Fiancé (3:1-5)

Shulamith in soliloquy

How I miss the one I love so deeply. I could not wait to see him. I thought to myself, "I must get up and find him. I will get up now and look around the streets and squares of the city for him. Surely I'll be able to find this one I love so much." But I could not find him. When the night watchmen of the city found me, I immediately asked them if they had seen this one I loved so deeply. But they had not. Yet no sooner did I pass from them than I found my beloved. I held on and on and would not let him go until I could bring him to my home. I still held on until my fearful anxieties left me and I felt peaceful once again. How hard it is to be patient! You women of the court, we must promise ourselves, by the gazelles and deer of the field, not to awaken love until love is pleased to awaken itself.

The Wedding Day (3:6-11)

Poet

What can this be coming from the outskirts of the city like columns of smoke, perfumed clouds of myrrh and frankincense, clouds of the scented powders of the merchant? Look! It is the royal procession with Solomon carried upon his lavish couch by his strongest servants. and take a look at all those soldiers around it! That is the imperial guard, the sixty mightiest warriors in the entire kingdom. Each one is an expert with his weapon and valiant in battle. Yet now each one has a sword at his side only for the protection of the King and his bride. Look at the luxurious couch Solomon is carried on. He has had it made especially for this day. He made its frame from the best timber of Lebanon. Its posts are made of silver, its back of gold, and its seat of royal purple cloth. And do you see its delicate craftsmanship! It reflects the skill of the women of the court who gave their best work out of love for the King and his bride. Let us all go out and look upon King Solomon wearing his elegant wedding crown. Let us go out and see him on the most joyful day of his life.

The Wedding Night (4:1-5:1)

King to Shulamith

You are so beautiful, my love, you are so beautiful. Your soft eyes are as gentle as doves from behind your wedding veil. Your hair is as captivating as the flowing movement of a flock descending a mountain at sunset. Your full and lovely smile is as cheerful and sparkling as pairs of young lambs scurrying up from a washing. And only a thread of scarlet could have outlined your lips so perfectly. Your cheeks flush with the redness of the pomegranate's hue. Yet you walk with dignity and stand with the strength of a fortress. Your necklace sparkles like the shields upon the fortress tower. But your breasts are a soft and gentle as fawns grazing among the lilies. And now at last, all through the night--until the day takes it first breath and the morning shadows flee from the sun--I will be a gazelle upon the hills of your perfumed breasts. You are completely and perfectly beautiful, my love, and flawless in every way. Now bring your thoughts completely to me, my love. Leave your fears in the far away mountains and rest in the security of my arms.

You excite me, my darling bride; you excite me with but a glance of your eyes, with but a strand of your necklace. How wonderful are your caresses, my beloved bride. Your love is more sweetly intoxicating than the finest wine. And the fragrance of your perfume is better than the finest spices. The richness of honey and milk is under your tongue, my love. And the fragrance of your garments is like the fragrance of the forests of Lebanon.

You are a beautiful garden fashioned only for me, my darling bride. Yes, like a garden kept only for me. Or like a fresh fountain sealed just for me. Your garden is overflowing with beautiful and delicate flowers of every scent and color. It is a paradise of pomegranates with luscious fruit, with henna blossoms and nard, nard and saffron, calamus and cinnamon with trees of frankincense, myrrh and aloes with all the choicest of spices. And you are pure as fresh water, yet more than a mere fountain. You are a spring for many gardens--a well of life-giving water. No, even more, you are like the fresh streams flowing from Lebanon which give life to the entire countryside.

Shulamith to King

Awake, O north wind, and come, wind of the south. Let your breezes blow upon my garden and carry its fragrant spices to my beloved. May he follow the enchanting spices to my garden and come in to enjoy its luscious fruit.

King to Shulamith

I have rejoiced in the richness of your garden, my darling bride.

I have been intoxicated by the fragrance of your myrrh and perfume. I have tasted the sweetness of your love like honey. I have enjoyed the sweetness of your love like an exquisite wine and the refreshment of your love like the coolness of milk.

Poet to couple

Rejoice in your lovemaking as you would rejoice at a great feast, O lovers. Eat and drink from this feast to the fullest. Drink, drink and be drunk with one another's love.

A Problem Arises (5:2-6:3)

Shulamith in soliloquy

I was half asleep when I heard the sound of my beloved husband knocking gently upon the door of our palace chamber. He whispered softly, "I'm back from the countryside, my love, my darling, my perfect wife." My only answer was a mumbled, "I've already gone to sleep, my dear." After all, I had already prepared for bed. I had washed my face and put on my old nightgown.

But then my beloved gently opened the door and I realized I really wanted to see him. I had hesitated too long though. By the time I arose to open the door, he had already walked away, leaving only a gift of my favorite perfume as a reminder of his love for me. Deep within my heart I was reawakened to my love for him. It was just that the fatigue and distractions of the day had brought my hesitating response. I decided to try to find him. I threw on my clothes, went outside the palace and began to call out to him.

But things went from bad to worse. The night watchmen of the city mistook me for a secretive criminal sneaking about in the night. They arrested me in their customarily rough style, then jerking my shawl from my head they saw the face of their newly found suspect--a "great" police force we have!

O, you women of the court, if you see my beloved King, please tell him that I deeply love him, that I am lovesick for him.

Women of the court to Shulamith

What makes your husband better than any other, O fairest of

women? What makes him so great that you request this so fervently of us?

Shulamith to women of the court

My beloved husband is strikingly handsome, the first to be noticed among ten thousand men. When I look at him, I see a face with a tan more richly golden than gold itself. His hair is as black as a raven's feathers and as lovely as palm leaves atop the stately palm tree. When I look into his eyes, they are as gentle as doves peacefully resting by streams of water. They are as pure and clear as health can make them.

When he places his cheek next to mine, it is as fragrant as a garden of perfumed flowers. His soft lips are as sweet and scented as lilies dripping with nectar. And how tender are his fingers like golden velvet when he touches me! He is a picture of strength and vitality. His stomach is as firm as a plate of ivory rippling with sapphires. And his legs are as strong and elegant as alabaster pillars set upon pedestals of fine gold. His appearance is like majestic Mt. Lebanon, prominent with its towering cedars.

But beyond all this, the words of his heart are full of charm and delight. He is completely wonderful in every way. This is the one I love so deeply, and this is the one who is my closest friend, O women of the palace court.

Women of the court to Shulamith

Where has your beloved gone, then O fairest among women? Where has he gone? We will help you find him.

Shulamith to women of the court

Oh, I know him well enough to know where he has gone. He likes to contemplate as he walks through the garden and cares for his special little flock among the lilies. I know him, for I belong to him and he belongs to me--this gentle shepherd who pastures his flock among the lilies.

The Problem Resolved (6:4-13)

King to Shulamith

My darling, did you know that you are as lovely as the city of

CHAPTER 7 — ROMANCE & SEX

Tirzah glittering on the horizon of night? No, more than that you are as lovely as the fair city of Jerusalem. Your beauty is as breathtaking as scores of marching warriors. (No, do not look at me like that now, my love; I have more to tell you.)

Do you remember what I said on our wedding night? It is still just as true. Your hair is as captivating as the flowing movement of a flock descending a mountain at sunset. Your lovely smile is as cheerful and sparkling as pairs of young lambs scurrying up from a washing. And your cheeks still flush with the redness of the pomegranate's hue.

King in soliloquy

The palace is full of its aristocratic ladies and dazzling mistresses belonging to the noblemen of the court. But my lovely wife, my dove, my flawless one, is unique among them all. And these ladies and mistresses realize it too. They too must praise her. As we approached them in my chariot, they eventually perceived that we were together again.

Women of the court to one another

Who is that on the horizon like the dawn, now fair as the moon but now plain and bright as the sun and as majestic as scores of marching warriors?

Shulamith in the chariot in soliloquy

I went down to the garden where I knew my King would be. I wanted to see if the fresh flowers and fruits of spring had come. I wanted to see if our reunion might bring a new season of spring love for my husband and me. Before I knew what happened, we were together again and riding past the palace court in his chariot. I can still hear them calling out, "Return, return O Shulamith; return that we may gaze at the beloved wife of the King."

King to Shulamith

How they love to look upon the incomparable grace and beauty of a queen.

In the Royal Bedroom (7:1-10)

CHAPTER 7   ROMANCE & SEX

King to Shulamith

How delicate are your feet in sandals, my royal prince's daughter! The curves of your hips are as smooth and graceful as the curves of elegant jewelry, perfectly fashioned by the skillful hands of a master artist. As delectable as a feast of wine and bread is your stomach--your navel is like the goblet of wine, and your stomach is the soft warm bread. Your breasts are as soft and gentle as fawns grazing among lilies, twins of a gazelle, and your neck is smooth as ivory to the touch. Your eyes are as peaceful as the pools of water in the valley of Heshbon, near the gate of the populous city.

Yet how strong you walk in wisdom and discretion. You are, indeed, as majestically beautiful as Mt. Carmel. Your long flowing hair is as cool and soft as silken threads draped round my neck, yet strong enough to bind me as your captive forever. How lovely and delightful you are, my dear, and how especially delightful is your love! You are as graceful and splendrous as a palm tree silhouetted against the sky. Yes, a palm tree--and your breasts are its luscious fruit.

I think I shall climb my precious palm tree and take its tender fruit gently into my hand. O my precious one, let your breasts be like the tender fruit to my taste, and now let me kiss you and breathe your fragrant breath. Let me kiss you and taste a sweetness better than wine.

Shulamith to King

And savor every drop, my lover, and let its sweetness linger long upon your lips, and let every drop of this wine bring a peaceful sleep.

Shulamith in soliloquy

I belong to my beloved husband and he loves me from the depths of his soul.

In the Countryside (7:11-8:14)

Shulamith to King

Spring's magic flowers have perfumed the pastel countryside

and enchanted the hearts of all lovers. Come, my precious lover; every delicious fruit of spring is ours for the taking. Let us return to our springtime cottage of towering cedars and cypresses where the plush green grass is its endless carpet and the orchards are its shelves for every luscious fruit. I have prepared a basketful for you, my love, to give you in a sumptuous banquet of love beneath the sky.

I wish we could pretend you were my brother, my real little brother. I could take you outside to play, and playfully kiss you whenever I wished. But then I could also take your hand and bring you inside and you could teach me and share with me your deep understanding of life. Then how I wish you would lay me down beside you and love me.

Shulamith to women of the court

I encourage you not to try to awaken love until love is pleased to awaken itself. How wonderful it is when it blossoms in the proper season.

Shulamith to King

Do you remember where our love began? Under the legendary sweetheart tree, of course, where every love begins and grows and then brings forth a newborn child, yet not without the pain of birth. Neither did our love begin without the pain, the fruitful pain of birth. O, my darling lover, make me your most precious possession held securely in your arms, held close to your heart. True love is as strong and irreversible as the onward march of death. True love never ceases to care, and it would no more give up the beloved than the grave would give up the dead.

The fires of true love can never be quenched because the source of its flame is God himself. Even were a river of rushing water to pass over it, the flame would yet shine forth. Of all the gifts in the world, this priceless love is the most precious and possessed only by those to whom it is freely given. For no man could purchase it with money, even the richest man in the world.

King to Shulamith

Do you remember how it was given to us?

CHAPTER 7 — ROMANCE & SEX

Shulamith to King

My love, I truly believe I was being prepared for it long before I even dreamed of romance. I remember hearing my brothers talking one evening. It was shortly after my father died, and they were concerned to raise me properly, to prepare me for the distant day of marriage. They were like a roomful of fathers debating about what to do with their only daughter. They finally resolved simply to punish and restrict me if I were promiscuous but to reward and encourage me if I were chaste. How thankful I am that I made it easy for them. I could see even when I was very young that I wanted to keep myself for the one dearest man in my life.

And then you came. And everything I ever wanted I found in you. There I was, working daily in the vineyard my brothers had leased from you. And you "happened" to pass by and see me. That's how our love began.

I remember when I worked in that vineyard that a thousand dollars went to you and two hundred dollars for the ones taking care of its fruit for you. Now I am your vineyard, my lover, and I gladly give the entire thousand dollars of my worth to you; I give myself completely, withholding nothing of my trust, my thoughts, my care, my love. But my dear King, let us not forget that two hundred dollars belongs to the ones who took care of the fruit of my vineyard for you. How thankful we must be to my family who helped prepare me for you.

King to Shulamith

My darling, whose home is the fragrant garden, everyone listens for the sound of your voice, but let me alone hear it now.

Shulamith to King

Hurry, then, my beloved. And again be like a gazelle or young stag on the hills of my perfumed breasts.*

---

*Taken from A SONG FOR LOVERS by S. Craig Glickman. c 1976 by Inter-Varsity Christian Fellowship of the USA and used by the author's permission.

Your love has given me great joy and encouragement...
(Philemon 7)

RELATIONSHIP SKILLS

I. **INTRODUCTION:** According to Martin Luther, "There is no more lovely, friendly and charming relationship, communion or company than a good marriage." This was not only a man of **fire**, but also a man of **family**. A man who knew the importance of relationship.

II. **GUIDELINES FOR CULTIVATING RELATIONSHIPS**

   A. Give _____ _____ to relationships. Proverbs 18:24b -- *...there is a friend who sticks closer than a brother.* John 15:15 -- *I no longer call you servants, because a servant does not know his master's business. Instead, I have called you friends, for everything that I learned from my Father I have made known to you.*

   1. **Here's a friendship test.** Answer these questions to yourself.

      a. Do you have at least one person nearby whom you can call on in times of personal distress?
      b. Do you have several people whom you can visit with little advance warning without apology?
      c. Do you have several people with whom you can share recreational activities?
      d. Do you have people who will lend you money or those who will care for you in practical

CHAPTER 8 — RELATIONSHIP SKILLS

ways if the need arises?

2. Love relationships do not just _____ -- we have to devote ourselves to them.

3. Give top priority to friendship with your _____. Of all earthly friendships, the one with our mate should be the best. God has given us to our mates as their **best friend**.

B. Develop _____. 1 Samuel 18:1 -- *After David had finished talking with Saul, Jonathan became one in spirit with David, and he loved him as himself.*

1. _____ promotes deep friendships. We need relationships in which we can be ourselves. We need someone (or a few) with whom we can be completely honest, and know that he/she will be honest and accepting in return. This is the kind of relationship that satisfies and lasts throughout our lives.

2. It is necessary to remove _____.

a. We leave them on because we fear rejection. We are afraid that if others saw the *real* us, they would be repelled.

b. Removal of our masks helps us know and accept ourselves. If we leave our masks on all the time, eventually **we** will forget what we really look like...how we really feel.

- **3. We are drawn to transparent people.** Real people are refreshing to be around. We are drawn to them. We have trouble, however, believing this same phenomena could be true of us. But it can! Others will be attracted to us if we allow ourselves the privilege of being real. Our mates especially will draw closer to us as we reveal ourselves to them.

C. Dare to _____ _____ about your feelings. 1 Samuel 20:17 -- *And Jonathan had David reaffirm his oath out of love for him, because he loved him as he loved himself.*

- **1. Appearing strong undermines sharing emotions.** Who said, "Real men don't cry"? John Wayne? Well, if he didn't say it, he certainly acted like it. He was the epitome of the "strong, silent type." But Jesus was never ashamed to show His feelings. When He was at His friend Lazarus' funeral, He wept openly (John 11).

- **2. Three magic words -- "I need you."** Don't be ashamed to share your feelings. Put aside your embarrassment and say to your mate, "I need you in my life." Everyone needs to feel needed. Let your mate know **how much** you need them.

- **3. Don't expect people to read your mind.**

D. Learn the _____ of love. John 12:3 -- *Then Mary took about a pint of pure nard, an* *expensive perfume; she poured it on Jesus' feet and wiped his feet with her hair. And the house was filled with the fragrance of the perfume.*

1. **Minister acts of love even when _____.** We don't have to **feel loving** to be **loving**. We can perform acts of love when we are tired. We can perform acts of love when we are grouchy. Anyone can give a back rub, a hug or a smile when they feel "lovey-dovey." But to give these acts of love when we **don't feel** like it...now **that** takes **love**!

2. **Recognize the significance of _____.** Giving a kiss when our partner comes home, reading to our children at bed time, singing a "love you" song to our children when they first awaken, kissing goodnight, holding each other close before falling asleep: repeated daily, these simple actions become rituals. They are extremely important to the bonding process. They are the mortar between the bricks.

3. **Give _____** -- not big, expensive gifts -- **thoughtful** gifts. Thoughtful gifts can cost little or no money. We can give an inexpensive item we've noticed our mate needs, or something free, like a back rub or a break from kitchen duties. Thoughtful gifts are **tangible evidence** of our love. We need to give them often.

E. **Don't let _____ control your life.**

1. **Criticism.** Hebrews 12:15 -- *See to it that no one misses the grace of God and that no **bitter root** grows up to cause trouble and defile many.* Philippians 2:14 -- *Do everything without complaining or arguing.*

   a. **Reasons to avoid criticism.** We have discussed criticism quite a bit, so you are already aware of how destructive it is. If it has gained a foothold in your life, ask the Lord to rip it out. You don't want it to control your life.

(1) It leads to and results from a negative mind-set. It makes us, and everyone around us, miserable.

(2) We are directed to fill our minds with positive things. Philippians 4:8 is worth repeating -- *Finally, brothers, whatever is true, whatever is noble, whatever is right, whatever is pure, whatever is lovely, whatever is admirable -- if anything is excellent or praiseworthy -- think about such things.*

Have you ever found a command in God's Word to "think of all the things your family and friends need to correct, and improve them with diligence"? We'd all be great at obeying that one, wouldn't we?

b. How to respond to criticism -- using the "PLAN" method.

(1) P -- Pray -- rather than defend. Our natural reaction is to defend ourselves. Bite your tongue, grit your teeth, cross your eyes -- do whatever your have to do, but don't allow yourself to **react**. Instead **respond -- pray**.

Example: Exodus 15:23-25 -- Moses and the Israelites at Marah: *When they came to Marah, they could not drink its water because it was bitter....So the people grumbled against Moses, saying, "What are we to drink?"* **Then Moses cried out to the Lord***....*

(2) L -- Listen and Learn. You won't want to listen. None of us likes to hear criticism. But we need to listen before we answer. Proverbs 18:13 -- *He who answers before listening -- that is his folly and his shame.*

(3) A -- Answer Positively:

- **(a)** Calmly and quietly as directed in Proverbs 15:1 -- *A gentle answer turns away wrath.*
- **(b)** Understand what your critic is saying. If you don't, ask questions.
- **(c)** Try to find truth (even a little) in what is said and immediately agree with all you possibly can.
- **(d)** Ask for your critic's help in finding a solution.

(4) N -- Note your critic's need. The criticism may actually stem from a problem within the critic himself. Don't try to "turn the tables" with such an accusation, but keep it in mind. Your critic may desperately need your understanding and prayer.

Example: Numbers 16:41-48 -- Moses, Aaron and the Israelites after Korah's rebellion: *The next day the whole Israelite community grumbled against Moses and Aaron....the Lord said to Moses, "Get away from this assembly so I can put an end to them at once....The plague had already started among the people, but Aaron **offered the incense and made atonement for them. He stood between the living and dead, and the plague** stopped.*

CHAPTER 8   RELATIONSHIP SKILLS

2. **Gossip**. In Romans 1:18, Paul declares that the *wrath of God is being revealed from heaven against all the godlessness and wickedness of men.* In the next fourteen verses, he describes these godless, wicked people, listing their horrible sins. Tucked in between murder and ruthlessness, is listed "gossip" and "slander." God wants to be sure we know exactly what He thinks about this **negative which can control our lives**. It is sin -- plain and simple. Gossip is defined as *idle talk and rumors*, especially about *the private affairs of others*.

    Some husbands and wives bad-mouth their mate and tell tales of their private lives to anyone who will listen -- especially extended family. It can destroy that mate's ability to form relationships with those who've heard the "gossip." And if what was said ever gets back to the slandered mate...! It also destroys the relationship between spouses, as the one gossiping tells and re-tells the negative stories. This type of gossip can be harder to acknowledge because it often takes the form of seeking help and comfort due to a "problem" spouse.

    It also occurs in idle banter and casual conversation, when a spouse tells about a "funny" incident ("You should have seen what my wife/husband did....") No wonder "gossip" is listed with murder, for it just as surely **destroys** lives and relationships, and perhaps does so more painfully than a knife or gun.

    a. **Why people gossip:**

         (1) To make themselves look better than the one they're speaking against.

         (2) To gain acceptance from those who are also judgmental toward the one they're speaking against.

(3) They follow a bad example.

(4) They are idle (1 Timothy 5:13).

b. Consequences of gossip:

(1) It separates friends, even intimate ones. Proverbs 16:28b -- *...a gossip separates close friends.*

(2) It wounds people and even destroys them.

(3) It instigates anger. Proverbs 25:23b -- *...a sly tongue brings angry looks.*

(4) It causes contention and strife. Proverbs 26:20 -- *Without wood a fire goes out; without gossip a quarrel dies down.*

c. Cures for gossip:

(1) Deal with others directly. Don't discuss the matter with others; go directly to the person involved. If a sin or personal offense is involved, use the confrontation process described in Matthew 18:15-17: first confront the Christian brother alone, then take 2 or 3 witnesses, and finally, if he still will not listen, bring him before the church.

(2) Refuse to listen to gossip. Proverbs 20:19 -- *A gossip betrays a confidence; so avoid a man who talks too much.* Simply refusing to listen may help others stop. If one person consistently attempts to draw you into gossip, consider confronting them.

(3) Be more open about your own weaknesses. Be vulnerable.

(4) Learn to love. Proverbs 10:12 -- *Hatred stirs up dissension, but love covers all*

wrongs.

(5) Ask the Lord to help you guard your tongue. Psalm 141:3 -- *Set a guard over my mouth, O Lord; keep watch over the door of my lips.*

3. **Manipulation.** Philippians 2:3 -- *Do nothing out of selfish ambition or vain conceit, but in humility consider others better than yourselves.*

   a. **Our demands and expectations lead to manipulation.**

      (1) **Our _____ of others** carry with them the specter of retribution, punishment or revenge when not fulfilled. Another name for unspoken threats is **manipulation**. Of course, we would never admit there was a threat hidden behind our demands, but if our mate or family does not measure up, we punish them with silence, sharp words or denials of pleasure.

      (2) **Our _____ of others** result in frustration and disappointment when not fulfilled. Our mate, family and friends will never be able to meet all our expectations. We stubbornly hang on to them, though, manipulating others to meet as many as possible.

      (3) **Our demands and expectations are _____-_____** and hurt us as well as others. When we place our demands and expectations on others, we make ourselves a target for defeat. Manipulation **does not work**. The people we try to manipulate catch on eventually. They resent and resist our control. In turn, we feel frustrated because we didn't get the results we wanted, and try even harder to manipulate others to meet our expectations

and demands. It's a vicious and counter-productive cycle.

b. Types of Manipulators: Check out these three categories of manipulators. Do you see yourself in any of them?

(1) The Take-Charge Manipulator -- These people think and act like they are in control.

How would you answer the following questions?

(a) Do we usually go to the restaurant or movie I prefer?

(b) Do I enjoy correcting factual errors in other people's conversation?

(c) Do I use humor to put down my mate or friends?

(d) Do I have to know more about a topic than others to feel comfortable discussing it?

(e) Do I flare-up in anger at those who don't do as I expect?

If you answered "Yes" to even two of these questions, you are a Take-charge manipulator. The Take-charger's weapon of choice is **fear**. Their sub-conscious line of thinking is, "Do what I want! If you don't, you'll **be** sorry."

(2) The Poor-Me Manipulator -- These are the sneaky manipulators...the martyrs.

Do you ever say, "Never mind, I'll do it myself." "Go ahead, take the last one. Don't bother about me." "I was looking forward to it, but, that's O.K., we'll do what you want. (sigh)"

If these statements sound like you, you are a Poor-me manipulator. The Poor-me's weapon of choice is **guilt**. Their sub-conscious line of thinking is, "You really should do what I want. If you don't, you'll **feel** sorry."

(3) The Need-to-be-needed Manipulator -- These folks make others dependent on them. They're doers, bustling over their loved ones, making themselves indispensable.

Do you feel that others **owe** you their gratitude? Are you hurt when you don't get the recognition you feel you deserve? Do you need to know that your husband or wife and children can not do without you?

If these reflect your feelings, then you are a Need-to-be-needed manipulator. The Need-to-be-needed's weapon of choice is **obligation**. Their sub-conscious line of thinking is, "Look what I do for you. You should do what I want because you **owe** me."

Manipulation is **deceit**. Instead of honestly saying what we want, we try to slip our expectations through the back door. We don't have time to go into all the ramifications of manipulation here. But we must make this clear: we are **all** guilty of manipulation. We must see it for the deceit that it is, and, with God's power, rid our lives of it.

F. Use you body to _____ **warmth.**
Luke 18:15 -- *People were also bringing babies to Jesus to have him touch them.*

1. **We all long to be touched.**

2. **Touching is a form of communication** that says, "I care about you. I'm listening. I'm interested."

CHAPTER 8   RELATIONSHIP SKILLS

A touch is stronger than verbal communication. It expresses comfort, acceptance, encouragement and love. Touch the people you love.

G. Be liberal with _____. Ephesians 4:29 -- *Do not let any unwholesome talk come out of your mouths, but only what is helpful for building others up according to their needs, that it may benefit those who listen.*

  1. Avoid _____ words: There are obvious words to avoid, such as lies (Eph 4:25), and bitter, angry, and malicious words (v 31). But there are other types of words that destroy, such as:

   a. _____ words: Proverbs 12:18 -- *Reckless words pierce like a sword.*

   b. _____ words: Proverbs 27:15 -- *A quarrelsome wife [or husband] is like a constant dripping on a rainy day.*

CHAPTER 8 — RELATIONSHIP SKILLS

    c. _____ words: Exaggerated generalizations that take the form of absolute statements are emotional clubs.

    d. _____ words: 1 Peter 3:9 -- *Do not repay evil with evil or insult with insult, but with blessing, because to this you were called so that you may inherit a blessing.*

2. **Practice _____ words:**

    a. _____ words: Proverbs 15:1 -- *A gentle answer turns away wrath.*

    b. _____ words: Proverbs 15:28 -- *The heart of the righteous weighs its answers.*

    c. _____ words: Philippians 1:3-5 -- *I thank my God every time I remember you. In all my prayers for all of you, I always pray with joy because of your partnership in the gospel from the first day until now.*

CHAPTER 8 — RELATIONSHIP SKILLS

  d. _____ **words:** Hebrews 10:25 -- *Let us not give up meeting together, as some are in the habit of doing, but let us encourage one another -- and all the more as you see the Day approaching.*

  e. _____ **words:** Philemon 7 -- *Your love has given me great joy and encouragement, because you, brother, have refreshed the hearts of the saints.*

  f. _____ **words:** 2 Timothy 1:5 -- *I have been reminded of your sincere faith, which first lived in your grandmother Lois and in your mother Eunice and, I am persuaded, now lives in you also.*

  g. _____ **words:** Luke 7:12-15 -- *As he approached the town gate, a dead person was being carried out -- the only son of his mother, and she was a widow....When the Lord saw her, his heart went out to her and he said, "Don't cry." Then he went up and touched the coffin....He said, "Young man, I say to you, get up!"...Jesus gave him back to his mother.*

H. Schedule time for _____ and _____. Proverbs 27:17 -- *As iron sharpens iron, so one man sharpens another.* Mark 6:31-32 -- *Then, because so many people were coming and going that they did not even have a chance to eat, he [Jesus] said to them, "Come with me by yourselves to a quiet place and get some rest."*

CHAPTER 8   RELATIONSHIP SKILLS

1. **Emotional intimacy takes time** -- time shared with one another in transparent communication. Our conversation should sharpen each other, like *iron sharpens iron*. Remember how you talked and talked while courting? You talked about everything, and excitedly informed your friends about the **interesting** person you had found.

2. **Our prescription for bonding:**

   1 X per week--a date together
   1 X per month--a long (over 4 hours) date
   1 X per quarter--an overnight away together
   1 X per 6 months-- a weekend away together

I. **Learn to _____.** James 1:19 -- *My dear brothers, take note of this: Everyone should be **quick to listen**, slow to speak and slow to become angry.* "Listen," as it is used here, means "to hear the **meaning** or **message** of the thing perceived" (Vine's *Expository Dictionary of New Testament Words*).

CHAPTER 8   RELATIONSHIP SKILLS

1. **Listen with your ears, eyes and body**...Lean toward the one speaking.
2. **Dispense advice sparingly.**
3. **Don't break confidences shared.**
4. **Give engaging responses.** "Uh-huh" and "Huh-uh" don't count.
5. **Show gratitude when loved ones confide in you.**
6. **Be patient with slow talkers.** Resist the urge to provide a word or finish a sentence.

J. **Allow people to _____.** Allow the people you love to make mistakes. Proverbs 17:17 -- *A friend loves at all times, and a brother is born for adversity.*

CHAPTER 8   RELATIONSHIP SKILLS

1. **Anatomy of failure:**

   a. **Fear of failure:** Are you open to change? Are you willing to take risks? Are you confident in decision making? Are you open to constructive criticism by others? If you answered "no" to any of these, **you** are afraid to fail. You are not alone. We are **all** afraid to fail.

   b. **Effects of failure:**

      (1) **We accelerate our performance.** We say to ourselves, "I'll show him. He'll never call me a failure again.!" Or, "No one will ever see me fail again."

      (2) **Or we quit.** We think, "What's the use? Why try, if I'm never going to get it right?"

      (3) **Both reactions sabotage us.**

      Ephesians 4:22-24 -- *You were taught, with regard to your former way of life, to **put off your old self**, which is being corrupted by its deceitful desires; to be **made new in the attitude of your minds**; and to **put on the new self**, created to be like God in true righteousness and holiness.*

2. **Freedom to fail.** Because we all know how hard it is to overcome feelings of failure, we need to stop encumbering our family and friends with our judgment and condemnation of their mistakes. Let's look at how we can repond in a positive, supportive manner, and give them the freedom to fail.

   a. **Give _____** -- Compassion says: "I'm not like those who have rejected you. I feel with you. My commitment to **unconditional**."

b. Give _____ -- We never need affirmation more than when we fail. And we never need to **give** it more than when our loved ones fail. Affirmation says: "You are not a dummy if you make a mistake. You are still worthy."

c. Give _____ -- Perspective says: "This failure isn't pleasant, but it is not monumental. It is solvable. God doesn't waste anything -- and He will somehow use this for good." (Romans 8:28)

d. Give _____ -- Disassociation says: "What you **did** failed, but **you** are not a failure."

e. Give _____ in Decision Making -- Encouragement says: "What do you think? I trust your opinion. And I'll back you, whatever you decide."

f. Give _____ -- Forgiveness says: "I won't reject you for your failure. I choose to forgive and accept you fully, just as you are; and I won't throw this back at you in the future."

Our loved ones make mistakes. They spill the coffee. They forget important things. They lock their keys in the car. They track mud in the house. They lose their jobs. They wreck the car. How are we going to respond to them? Will we heap guilt and recrimination on them? Or will we give them freedom to fail? Ecclesiastes 4:9-10 -- *Two are better than one, because they have a good return for their work:* ***If one falls down, his friend can help him up.*** *But pity the man who falls and has no one to help him up!*

III. CONCLUSION:

Once upon a time, there was a beautiful Princess who married her Prince Charming. They were so much in love, they spent every possible minute together. They talked for hours about their hopes and dreams for the future. They grew to know each other so well, they could almost tell what the other was thinking. Their love was marked by kind deeds and thoughtful gestures, and never was there a critical or demanding word spoken between them, but only words of praise. As they walked hand in hand through the village streets, the villagers would exclaim, "What a perfect couple!" But they were so intent on their own conversation, they hardly noticed when others interrupted. The Prince never fussed when the Princess forgot to press his royal robes, and she would simply smile and wink when he tracked mud on the royal carpets.

The Prince worked very hard as he climbed the royal ladder of success, and spent more and more time on his many duties. With the Prince away so much, the Princess lavished her time on the little prince and princesses, especially as they became active in the royal Little League and Archery Club. Whenever the Prince returned home from his princely work, exceedingly tired and tense, he would proclaim, in his princely way, that he wished not to be disturbed. Then he would prop his feet on his footstool and read the Royal Gazette. The Princess, when she wasn't transporting the little prince and princesses hither and yon in the royal carriage, threw herself into her royal duties of charity. The Prince and Princess did not spend much time together any more. By the time they entered their royal bed chamber, they were too tired to talk and listen to one another about hopes and dreams. After a while, they no longer held hands as they walked. But, since they took walks together so seldom, the lack of touch went almost unnoticed. Their kind deeds and thoughtful gestures were forgotten, replaced by words of criticism and sarcasm. The Prince now demands his royal robes be pressed and ready every morning by 7:00. And the Princess frets greatly over the prince's thoughtless messes. How sad! What has happened to the Prince and Princess' "happy ever after"?

CHAPTER 8   RELATIONSHIP SKILLS

IV. Group Discussion

A. Praise:

  1. List some situations where destructive words are commonly used.
  2. How could constructive words work in these same situations?

B. Manipulation:

  1. What are some situations where you have seen or used a manipulative technique? Try to think of a situation to illustrate each of the 3 categories: Take-Charge, Poor-Me, and Need-to-be-needed.
  2. Using the same situations, discuss how the truth could be spoken in love and manipulative techniques not used.

C. Allowing Your Mate to Fail

  1. Relate a time when you were given the needed compassion, affirmation etc. by your mate or someone else when you failed.

V. COUPLE SHARING

1. Write a list of 10 qualities you like about your mate. Review all of them together as a couple. Keep your list as a guide from which to compliment your mate.

2. Which of the relationship guidelines do you most want to apply? Why?

3. When your spouse, or other people, fail, which of the following freedoms do you have the most difficulty extending to them: Compassion, affirmation, perspective, disassociation, encouragement in decision-making or forgiveness? Why?

I Press on toward the goal....
(Phil. 3:14)

COUPLE GOAL SETTING

I. **INTRODUCTION:** Most people think of goals in a business context, but they are essential in our personal lives as well.

II. **GOALS -- _____ ARE THEY?**

  A. **Purposes, Objectives and Goals:** Purpose is the over-all general direction we want to take. We say, "Our purpose in life is...." It's very broad and far-reaching. An objective is still rather general, but is more narrow than "purpose." Within one purpose, we might have three or four objectives. When we speak of goals, however, we are being **specific**. That's what we want to be in this chapter -- specific.

  B. **Elements of a good goal:** Goals must be...

  1. _____

  2. _____ enough to be measurable

  3. _____ limited

CHAPTER 9 — GOAL SETTING

III. IS GOAL SETTING _____?

A. We are to "count the cost" of projects and involvements: Luke 14:28:30 -- *Suppose one of you wants to build a tower. Will he not first sit down and estimate the cost to see if he has enough money to complete it? For if he lays the foundation and is not able to finish it, everyone who sees it will ridicule him, saying, 'This fellow began to build and was not able to finish.'*

B. Our goals must please the Lord. 2 Corinthians 5:9 -- *So we make it our goal to please him, whether we are at home in the body or away from it.*

C. We are to "care for our own." 1 Timothy 5:8 -- *If anyone does not provide for his relatives, and especially for his immediate family, he has denied the faith and is worse than an unbeliever.*

IV. GOAL-SETTING IN NINE _____ OF LIFE

A. Areas defined:

1. **Marriage goals** -- Goals that affect the husband-wife relationship.

2. **Spiritual goals** -- Goals that affect our relationship with God and church.

3. **Parenting/Family goals** -- Goals that affect our relationships with our children or relatives.

4. **Vocational goals** -- Goals that affect our career pursuits.

5. **Physical goals** -- Goals that affect our bodies.

CHAPTER 9 — GOAL SETTING

   6. **Financial goals** -- Goals that affect our monetary welfare.

   7. **Recreational goals** -- Goals that affect our fun and relaxation pursuits.

   8. **Emotional goals** -- Goals that the affect the well-being of our mind, heart and souls.

   9. **Social goals** -- Goals that affect interpersonal relationships or civic welfare.

B. **Sample goals for each area:**

   1. **Marriage goal** -- "Plan a date for the entire day for our anniversary at least three weeks ahead of the day."

   2. **Spiritual goal** -- "Have devotions with my spouse at least four times per week for 15-20 minutes each time."

   3. **Parenting/Family goal** -- "Plan a date with each of my children for 2 hours apiece within the next 2 months."

   4. **Vocational goal** -- "Start classes for my Master's Degree by September of this year."

   5. **Physical goal** -- "Take a 30 minute walk at least 4 times per week after dinner, starting this week."

   6. **Financial goal** -- "Collect a savings account of $2000 for emergencies by November of this year."

   7. **Recreational goal** -- "Plan a two week summer vacation for this summer. Have planning done and reservations made by June 1."

   8. **Emotional goal** -- "Read one book strictly for

pleasure each month."

   9. Social goal -- "Have one couple in our home for a social time at least once per month, starting next month."

C. **Constructing your goals:**

Using the goal-setting worksheet, write **one goal in each area**. Use the samples listed in **B** as a guide. Remember: be realistic, be specific, and set a time limit.

V. WORKING WITH THE GOAL WORKSHEETS.

1. **Place a star (*)** beside the **4 goals** you feel are most important to your marriage. Then number them in order of importance -- 1 through 4.

2. **Place a zero (0)** beside the **two goals** you would be willing to live without if it were absolutely necessary. These, of course, should be chosen from the remaining five goals. This does not eliminate these two goals. It is simply a tool to help you decide which are the least important.

3. **Place a dollar sign ($)** beside each goal that costs money.

4. **Place a "P"** beside those influenced by your parents, from either a negative or positive point of view. Positive: "I want to have family devotions just like my parents had with me." Or negative: "I want to have family devotions because my parents never had them, and I don't want our children to miss out."

5. **Place an "S"** beside those you think your spouse has written down. No peeking!

6. **Place a cross (+)** beside the goals you feel God considers important. You might mark only a few or all of them. Think carefully and answer honestly.

7. **Write a paragraph** about one of your goals on the

worksheet. Choose whichever one you wish and write a few sentences explaining the importance of that goal to your marriage.

VI. CONCLUSION

Knowing what you're aiming at isn't enough. You must take the steps needed to "reach the target."

VII. COUPLE SHARING

1. Compare your goals. Which ones are the same?

2. Compare and discuss your four most important goals. Why are they the most important? Would you like them to be mutual goals?

3. Together, choose one goal to work on mutually. Discuss a plan of action to accomplish it.

4. When you get home, tape both goal sheets to the front of your refrigerator or bathroom mirror. Don't stick them in a drawer and forget about them. Keep your goals (and your goal sheets) in sight.

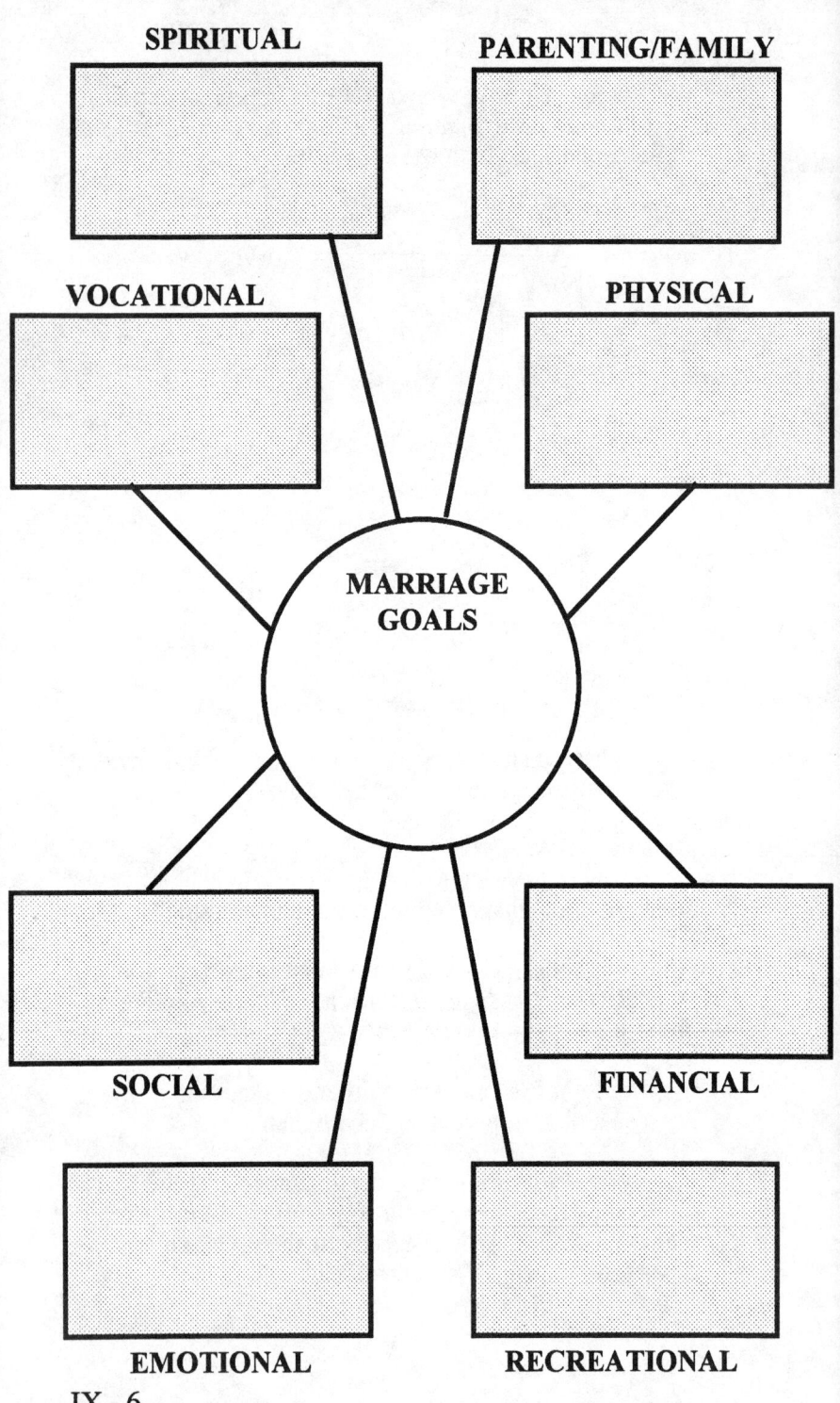

Many waters cannot quench love, neither can the floods drown it....
(Song of Sol. 8:7 KJV)

COMMITMENT

I. **INTRODUCTION:** Is commitment "...as long as we both shall live"? or "...as long as we both shall love"? Both are true in God's design for He wants us to love each other our whole lives.

II. **COMMITMENT PROCESS:**

   A. **The parts of a "whole _____":
   Intellect, emotions and will.**

   This is pretty standard information. We have an **intellect** -- our mind which affects our behavior because of its thought processes. We also have **emotions** -- our feelings which pull us in a particular direction. And thirdly, we have a **will** -- our power to act or choose with purpose. These three parts make up our personality: how we think and respond to life.

   B. **Our _____ can act despite our emotions.**

   Examples in Psalms:

   1. **Psalm 42:5,6** -- *Why are you downcast, O my soul? Why so disturbed within me? Put your hope in God, for I will yet praise him, my Savior and my God. **My soul is downcast within me; therefore I will remember you** from the land of the Jordan, the heights of Hermon -- from Mount Mizar.* **Because** David was downcast, he chose to

X - 1

remember the Lord. His emotions would have kept him down; but his will, with help from his intellect, chose to look up to God.

2. **Psalm 69:1-3** -- *Save me, O God, for the waters have come up to my neck. I sink in the miry depths, where there is no foothold. I have come into the deep waters; the floods engulf me. I am worn out calling for help; my throat is parched. My eyes fail, looking for my God.* How is David feeling? To borrow our son-in-law's expression: "He's lower than a snake's belly in a wagon rut." You can't get much lower than that. But by verse 29, he exercises his will despite his feelings. *I am in pain and distress; may your salvation, O God, protect me.* ***I will praise God's name*** *in song and* ***glorify him*** *with thanksgiving (69:29-30).*

3. **Psalm 22:1-2, 6** -- *My God, my God, why have you forsaken me? Why are you so far from saving me, so far from the words of my groaning? O my God, I cry out by day, but you do not answer, by night, and am not silent....I am a worm and not a man, scorned by men and despised by the people.* Have you ever felt **so low**, you called yourself a **worm**? Maybe a worm's belly in a wagon rut is even **lower** than a snakes. But again, by verse 22, David makes a **decision** to trust God...**his will over-rides his emotions**. *I will declare your name to my brothers; in the congregation* ***I will*** *praise you. You who fear the Lord, praise him! All you descendants of Jacob, honor him! Revere him, all you descendants of israel!* (22:22-23) David not only chooses to trust and praise God despite his emotions, he **encourages his friends** to do the same.

C. The _____ to decide.

Simply **knowing** we don't need **to feel** in order **to do** doesn't change our lives, does it? We can know this

absolutely, and still **react** to circumstances with our emotions instead of our intellect and will. We must **choose** to **respond** instead of **react** to circumstances and people.

III. LOVE IS A DECISION.

A. To love is a _____.

In the three following verses, **God commands us to love**. Now, He never gives us commands we are not capable of obeying. So "love" must be more than a feeling, for how could God command us to **"feel"**? Love is more than emotions, it is a **decision**...a decision to obey God's command.

1. Husbands are commanded to _____ _____. Ephesians 5:25 -- *Husbands, love your wives, just as Christ loved the church and gave himself up for her.*

2. We are all commanded to _____ _____ _____. Galatians 5:14 -- *The entire law is summed up in a single command: "**Love your neighbor** as yourself."*

3. We are commanded to _____ _____ _____. 1 John 4:21 -- *And he has given us this command: Whoever loves God must also **love his brother**.*

B. To love is a _____ _____ -- Titus 2:3-4 -- *Likewise, teach the older women to be reverent in the way they live, not to be slanderers or addicted to much wine, but to teach what is good. Then **they can train the younger women to love** their husbands and children.*

C. We can love despite contrary _____ or the absence of emotion. 1 Corinthians 13:7-8 -- *It [love] always protects, always trusts, always hopes, always perseveres. Love never fails.*

D. The need for _____. Ecclesiastes 5:4,5 -- *When you make a vow to God, do not delay in fulfilling it. He has no pleasure in fools; fulfill your vow. It is better not to vow than to make a vow and not fulfill it.* What does God call us if we make a vow and don't keep it? Fools! He calls us fools! God takes vows very seriously. When we promised to "love, honor and cherish" our mates, we made a **vow** of commitment to one another and to God.

NOTE: We know that some of you are in second marriages. The first vows you took have been broken, perhaps not by your choice. We are not speaking of the past. The only thing we can do about the past is **forgive** and **be forgiven** for it. We trust you have dealt with God about that and have accepted His forgiveness and forgiven those who hurt you. If you have, you are now free to fulfill your vow with your present mate, and are held responsible by God to do so.

CHAPTER 10   **COMMITMENT**

1. **Commitment is a decision to** _____.
Genesis 2:22-24 -- *Then the Lord God made a woman from the rib he had taken out of the man, and he brought her to the man. The man said, "This is now bone of my bones and flesh of my flesh; she shall be called 'woman,' for she was taken out of man." For this reason a man will leave his father and mother and **be united** to his wife, and they will become **one flesh**.* We like the way the King James Version translates "united:" *a man will leave his father and mother and **cleave** unto his wife.* God's command for married couples is to "leave and cleave." We must **leave** all other ties that hold us, so that we can freely bond to our mate.

4. **The necessity to make a commitment**. It was important to our relationship that we make a **verbal restatement** of our commitment to one another. And we believe it is important for your relationship as well. We know you made vows at the altar just like we did. But now you know more of what they mean, so your recommitment will mean more than your original one.

IV. **MINISTRY VERSUS MANIPULATION:** Ministry is our commitment to **love in shoe leather**. When we minister to our mate, we are focusing on them and their needs.

     A. **Because only Christ can meet our** _____ _____, **we must turn to Him, not our** _____, **for the satisfaction of our personal needs for** _____ **(love) and** _____ **(meaning/purpose).**

CHAPTER 10 — COMMITMENT

Romans 5:8 -- *But God demonstrates his own love for us in this: While we were still sinners, Christ died for us.*

B. Because Christ satisfies our needs, we are _____ to minister to the needs of our mate, instead of _____ our mate to meet our needs. Galatians 5:13 -- *You, my brothers, were called to be free. But do not use your freedom to indulge the sinful nature; rather, serve one another in love.*

C. How to become a minister to our mate: We have freedom in Christ to **become** ministers, so now we must learn **how** to be ministers.

　1. Make a _____ to minister to your partner's needs with a _____ _____. 1 Timothy 6:18 -- *Command them to do good, to be rich in good deeds, and to be generous and willing to share.*

　2. Determine to become more _____ of your partner's needs. Philippians 2:4 -- *Each of you should look not only to your own interests, but also to the interests of others.*

CHAPTER 10 — COMMITMENT

   3. Recognize that God Himself has _____ you to minister to your mate's needs in a unique way. Hebrews 13:20-21 -- *May the God of peace...equip you with everything good for doing his will, and may he work in us what is pleasing to him, through Jesus Christ....*

V. **CONCLUSION:** Commitment is not some nebulous feeling. It is not a one-time decision somewhere in the past. It is not theoretical. It is real -- every day. It is real in the decisions you make every day. It is real when you feel like it...and when you don't feel like it.

CHAPTER 10   COMMITMENT

A. Personal illustration

Bette: It was the night before my fortieth birthday. Harold and the kids were dishing out some heavy duty teasing about my big 4-0 when the telephone rang...so innocently. We didn't know that phone call would change our lives forever. I had a biopsy the week before on a growth beside my breastbone. The surgeon called that night to tell us I had two months to live. First, however, he wanted to surgically remove the grapefruit-size tumor, my breastbone, the ribs the tumor had grown through, my left breast and the sack from around my heart. Then somehow he was going to sew me back together so I could die in one piece. From my biopsy, the pathologists had diagnosed me with Malignant Thymoma...and no one lives with that.

Our family huddled together, crying and praying. Our children were only 13, 15 and 17. We held them close and thought about how I might not live to watch them grow up. We were exhausted, our minds and bodies drained by a great dread. Harold and I clung to each other in the middle of the bed, not expecting to fall asleep. But we did. We immediately drifted into sweet, dreamless sleep.

We didn't know it then, but many friends had been called by our Pastor and a close friend and were praying for us all night. Finally, at four a.m., they felt peace and were able to sleep. They carried -- literally carried -- our burden all night so that we could rest.

Harold: We awoke refreshed at four a.m., the time our Christian friends were able to sleep. We've since kidded them that they should have prayed 'til at least 6:00.

After we awoke, we lay there in each other's arms and began to sing hymns and choruses, one after another, as they popped into our minds. And we read God's Word -- mostly Psalms -- claiming the promises of comfort and help and blessing.

CHAPTER 10 — COMMITMENT

When I called, you answered me....Though I walk in the midst of trouble, you preserve my life....The Lord will fulfill His purpose for me.... (Psalm 138:3-8). Great and true promises made by a loving God to millions of believers through the ages, but that morning they were for us alone. We had begun GTO Family Ministries just two years before. It was our niche -- our calling. Was this to be the end of it? It couldn't be, not if helping couples **was** His purpose for us. We knew that somehow -- somehow -- we were going to make it through this. How? We didn't know. But the terrible dread that had overwhelmed us the night before was gone, and in its place God had given peace.

Bette: Peace. A difficult thing to keep in the days that followed -- days filled with doctors, hospitals, tests, second opinions, third opinions. After the second opinion agreed with the first, I was sent for a consultation with the plastic surgeon who was to sew me back together after surgery. He recommended I see one more doctor, a surgical oncologist at University Hospital (University of California, San Diego). He called him then and there and arranged an almost impossible-to-get appointment for me the next day. That appointment resulted in more pathologists examing my biopsy block and diagnosing me with Hodgkin's Disease, not Malignant Thymoma. Hodgkin's Disease is cancer of the lymph system and is treated with chemotherapy and radiation, not surgery.

We were ecstatic when we heard the new diagnosis. Imagine being happy to discover you have Hodgkin's disease! But it is perspective. My chances, from a medical point of view, soared from 0% to 50%. I remember stopping at the grocery store on our way home, and as we were getting out of the car, we spotted a good friend across the parking lot. I waved my arms excitedly and shouted, "Lynne, I've got Hodgkin's Disease! I've got Hodgkins Disease!" Like I said, it's perspective.

Harold: Then we started chemotherapy...every two weeks for nine long months. And with every month, every treatment, Bette grew weaker. After a few months, it became too difficult for her to crawl up and down stairs more than once or twice a day. Her nausea and pain seemed to worsen with each treatment.

Bette: My hair fell out by hand fulls. Soon, even my face looked bald. I felt so useless and ugly. I didn't feel human, much less feminine. But Harold would take my hand and say, "You're beautiful." I'd cry, "How can you even look at me? How can you still love me?" He'd smile and reply, "Hey, if you can love me bald, I can love you bald."

For almost a year, I could only take; I could not give. I couldn't iron his shirts, couldn't fix a decent meal, couldn't feel or look sexy -- but Harold still showed me he loved me. He held a pan under my chin for me to throw up in, he let me cry on his shoulder, he made me talk about how I felt, and he reminded me regularly that I was still valuable. I knew beyond a shadow of a doubt that he was fully committed to me and to our marriage. And I knew he loved me -- not in some ethereal way but in every day, nitty-gritty ways. We learned in the trenches what commitment and love and ministering really mean.

B. The most important thing on earth: our commitment to oneness.

We must nurture our relationship **now** -- every day. We must decide to put love and ministry **into practice -- every day**. The hard times will come. If you haven't already found that out, you will. And if you're not in the process of learning to put love into action, those hard times are going to pry you apart. Don't wait for circumstances to get better. Start learning to love and minister to each other **today**.

CHAPTER 10 COMMITMENT

VI. GROUP DISCUSSION QUESTIONS

1. If you really treated love as a decision and not just an emotion, how would your behavior change? Give some practical examples.

2. Why is it easier to manipulate our partners rather than minister to them?

3. Case Study

    Fred enters his home after a long day at work. His automatic, unplanned, and perhaps unconscious goal likely involves a desirable response from his wife Joan, perhaps a friendly greeting, a warm hug, or a prepared dinner. Suppose she welcomes him by asking, "Why are you so late? You said you'd be home by six and it's nearly seven."

    Fred feels angry at Joan. He feels like retorting with, "Hey, thanks for the warm welcome! Sure is nice to come home!"

    What should he do? Some of his options are (1) to express his anger, (2) to defend his late arrival, (3) simply to ignore Joan's comment and wash up for dinner, or (4) to soothe her with a warm embrace. Does he have other options? What would the loving thing to do be? What would you do if you were Fred? If you were Joan?

CHAPTER 10 COMMITMENT

VII. COUPLE QUESTIONS

1. Ways I tend to 　　　　Ways I could
   manipulate my partner:　minister instead:

2. When you are alone together, sit down, facing each other, and declare basically the following to each other. "I love you. I am devoted to you. I'm committed to you and to our marriage. I will honor and cherish you and remain faithful to you until death separates us. And if it were ever necessary, I would lay down my life for you. (Spend some time to put the above in your own words.)

3. I recognize that only Christ can meet your deepest needs, but I want to minister to you more than I do. Give me some suggestions as to how I can be a better minister to you. I want to meet more of your needs.

A cord of three strands is not quickly [easily] broken. (Eccl. 4:12)

SPIRITUAL INTIMACY

I. INTRODUCTION

If you are one of those couples who has never given Spiritual Intimacy much thought, this is your **wake up call**. Not a call for **perfection**, but for **progress**. And Spiritual Intimacy is the means to that progress. Would it surprise you to know that you and your spouse are **commanded** to be spiritually intimate, and that you have been given the **power** and **capacity** to be so? In fact, if you want to feel as close as you have always longed to feel as a married couple, then growing together in spiritual intimacy is an absolute necessity in your marriage.

What is Spiritual Oneness? We can't give you a one line definition; it's more complicated than that. In fact, spiritual intimacy has at least seven elements that interweave in an intricate design to form a way of life. You see, it is a **process--not an event**...a journey--not the name of the destination.

II. SPIRITUAL INTIMACY

A. What is it?

1. Shared _____ and _____ in Life

Paul declares through the Holy Spirit, *If [since] you have any encouragement from being united with Christ, if [since] any comfort from his love, if [since] any fellowship with the Spirit, if [since] any tenderness and compassion, then make my joy complete by being like-minded, having the same love, being one in spirit and purpose* (Philippians 2:1,2). Think about it. If we as the body of Christ are commanded to be one in spirit and purpose, how much more are you as a Christian couple to be one in spirit and purpose? If you as a couple do not share a common goal in life, how will you ever reach it? If you are on different roads, headed in divergent directions, then it is no wonder you do not feel close.

This is the first step in your spiritual intimacy journey: make sure you are taking the trip together. And, by the way, don't forget to pack your suitcases. Fill them with *encouragement* and *comfort* for one another, *fellowship* with the Spirit, *tenderness, compassion* and *love* just as Philippians 2 said. Keep them handy because you are going to need to pull them out and use them everyday.

2. Sharing the _____ and _____

Paul commands in Colossians, *Let the word of Christ dwell in you richly as you teach and admonish one another with all wisdom....* (Colossians 3:16). All this is saying is that we should read God's Word together and talk about it. This is beneficial in any of our relationships, but it is especially beneficial to the relationship between two believing spouses. They become partners encouraging one another along the road, reminding each other of the reality of God's Word in their lives. Not preaching, mind you, or beating each other around the head and shoulders with Scripture verses. But allowing God's Word, richly living in us, to change us into the image of His Son, and then sharing that change with our partners.

In Matthew 18:19-20, we read, *Again, I tell you that if two of you on earth agree about anything you ask for, it will be done for you by my Father in heaven. For where two or three come together in my name, there am I with them.* We can't explain how this works, we just know it does. In some mysterious way, when the two of you pray together, you are promised power in prayer. In some special way, Jesus is there with you and your partner. What a promise! But what a waste if you two are not praying together!

3. Shared _____ in Christ

You and your mate are walking down the road together. You're sharing with him/her all that good stuff from Philippians 2 you packed in your suitcase: comfort, love, tenderness, compassion, etc. You are reading the Scriptures and praying together as you walk. Jesus Christ has become someone easy to talk about. Now, as you walk along, you find yourself growing stronger spiritually, with more energy and stamina than before. This, dear friends, *should* be a natural progression.

But what should be natural to the "new creature in Christ" is often radically **un-natural** to our "old self." Our hearts want to obey God's life-giving principles of love and compassion, but they usually end up in the bottom of our suitcase. And what are those **old rags** on top? Bitterness and criticism. Everytime we open our suitcase, we must make a conscious choice to push aside the rags and rummage for the love and compassion. But each time we choose love and compassion makes it easier to find them in our suitcase the next time. For **God is at work** within us. He is the One who helps us discard the rags and choose the garments of righteousness as described in Philippians 2.

Hebrews 10:24 -- *And let us consider how we may spur one another on toward love and good deeds.*

As you continue down the road together -- *allowing* one another to grow -- try applying Ephesians 5:19 to your daily journey. *Speak to one another with psalms, hymns and spiritual songs. Sing and make music in your heart to the Lord.*

When we sing songs together like

You are my hiding place

You always fill my heart

With songs of deliverance

Whenever I am afraid

I will trust in you

What do you think that does to our faith as we remind ourselves in song of God's faithfulness? That must be why God commanded us to do it!

CHAPTER 11   SPIRITUAL INTIMACY

4. Shared _____ Even When It's Tough

God says, *Carry each other's burdens, and in this way you will fulfill the law of Christ* (Galatians 6:2). Picture yourselves walking along the road together. One of you is carrying a heavy bucket. The other picks up a sturdy stick and runs it through the bucket handle. You can each carry the bucket now by holding the ends of the stick. That's **how** *to carry each other's burdens.* When two hearts carry the same load, the burden is only half as heavy!

How beautifully this is depicted in Ecclesiastes 4:9-12. *Two are better than one, because they have a good return for their work: If one falls down, his friend can help him up. But pity the man who falls and has no one to help him up! Also, if two lie down together, they will keep warm. But how can one keep warm alone? Though one may be overpowered, two can defend themselves. A cord of three strands is not quickly [easily] broken.* Yes, there will be stones in the road, and you are going to stumble over some of them. But you are called to stick together, and help each other over or through the rough spots.

CHAPTER 11   SPIRITUAL INTIMACY

You will be strong enough to hold each other up because you have been growing together on this spiritual journey. The *cord of three strands* -- you, your mate, and your God -- is **strong enough** to hold you up.

Have you discovered any stones in your road? Big, aren't they? At times they are overwhelming. If you haven't stumbled across any yet, believe us, you will.

Always keep in mind this great truth: there are **three** of you walking together on this road, not just two. And when you get too weary to take another step, there's a Third Person, Jesus Christ Himself, Who is strong enough to hold both of you up until you can face the next step together. *A cord of three strands [really] is not quickly or easily broken.*

5. Shared _____

Now you are ready for the fifth ingredient of spiritual oneness: shared ministry. Have you ever thought about how important the number "2" is to God? Think about it. Many times throughout Scripture, God sends two people or two angels to accomplish His purposes: two angels to Abraham, two angels to Lot, two disciples to fetch the Palm Sunday colt, two angels at the empty tomb, and the 72 disciples sent out two-by-two, just to name a few.

Why does God minister so often by two's? Ecclesiastes 4:9-12 explained it. When there's a job to be done, two can usually handle it better, because they help each other through to the finish. There is a couple in Scripture that depicts this in a beautiful way. Their names are Aquila and Priscilla. Let's follow them through the Bible and learn from their example.

Acts 18 -- *After this, Paul left Athens and went to Corinth. There he met a Jew named Aquila, a native of Pontus, who had recently come from Italy with his wife Priscilla, because Claudius had ordered all the Jews to leave Rome. Paul went to see them, and because he was a tentmaker as they were, he stayed and worked with them...So Paul stayed for a year and a half teaching them the word of God...Then he left the brothers and sailed for Syria accompanied by Priscilla and Aquila...They arrived at Ephesus where Paul left Priscilla and Aquila...Meanwhile a Jew named Apollos...came to Ephesus...He began to speak boldly in the synagogue. When Priscilla and Aquila heard him, they invited him to their home and explained to him the way of God more adequately.*

I Corinthians 16:19 -- *The churches in the province of Asia send you greetings. Aquila and Priscilla greet you warmly in the Lord, and so does the church that meets at their house.*

Romans 16:3,4 -- *Greet Priscilla and Aquila, my fellow workers in Christ Jesus. They risked their lives for me. Not only I but all the churches of the Gentiles are grateful to them.*

Ministering together may have an additional aspect as well. One of you may teach a Sunday School class or lead a boy's or girl's club or whatever. But you can still be ministering as a team by being involved in one another's service.

What have Priscilla and Aquila shown us about shared ministry?

- a. **Their home was open and available for ministry to others** -- both to individuals like Apollos and to groups like the church that met there.
- b. **They shared together in both ministries** -- The passages don't say that Aquila took Apollos aside, nor that he alone led the church in their home -- it mentions them **together** in **both** cases.
- c. **They were willing to move for the sake of ministry to others.** **People** were always more important than **things** to them.
- d. **And finally, they submitted their ministry to Paul's authority and guidance** as we should to our church leaders.

6. **Shared Hope of _____ Together With Christ**

    1 Thessalonians 4:17-18--*After that, we who are still alive and are left will be caught up with them in the clouds to meet the Lord in the air. And so we will be with the Lord forever. Therefore encourage each other with these words.* And that is exactly what we want to do: encourage you with this element of Spiritual intimacy.

    We have also been given this hope so that we will purify ourselves. *But we know that when he appears, we shall be like him, for we shall see him as he is. Everyone who has this hope in him purifies himself, just as he is pure* (1 John 3:2b-3). If eventually we are going to be pure in heaven, why bother purifying ourselves now? Verse 2 starts with, *Now we are children of God....*
    That's why we need, and are commanded, to be purifying ourselves **now** while we wait for Him to appear.

When we stand before Him as His children, He will be looking for a **family resemblance**. Will we meet Him with joy? Or will it be with shame, not because we **could not** put on the likeness of Christ, but because we **would not**.

God holds us responsible for whether or not we act like Him **inside** our front doors. Whatever you do, don't sit by and let the day come when you meet your mate in heaven and must hang your head in regret and shame because you would not let the Lord *conform you to the likeness of His Son* in your home (Romans 8:29). If you are not acting like Jesus to your mate, then it is time to start allowing the Holy Spirit to change you. *Purify yourselves* because you are going to spend all of eternity together *with the Lord.*

7. Sharing at the _____ of Our Being

Remember the second element of Spiritual intimacy? The one about praying together? After travelling on this road for a while and learning to pray together, you will find it is easier to pray about everything with one another. As you begin to pray about your hopes and dreams and aspirations, as well as your failures and doubts and sin, you will become more and more open with the Lord and with each other. You will become less and less afraid to show the real you.

Paul states in Acts 24:16, *So I strive always to keep my conscience clear before God and man.* Can you see how this happens when you and your mate are consistently praying together? When you keep your conscience clear before God, it will also be clear before "man" -- that is, your mate. Couple prayer is actually a three-way conversation which can become the most precious and intimate time of your lives.

Another verse to consider concerning this intimate kind of sharing is James 5:16. *Therefore confess your sins to each other and pray for each other so that you may be healed....* Many couples are cheating themselves out of personal, emotional healing by refusing to be real and honest with their mates.

B. What are the benefits?

1. TRUST:

Trust is developed in our relationship as we discover we can trust our mate to be honest with us, and as we come to feel that our love is safe with them. All the steps in our Spiritual Intimacy journey will **lead** to trust. We can't be honest with God without being honest with our mates when we're growing in the three-way relationship that Spiritual oneness creates.

2. BONDING:

Secondly, there will be significant **bonding** between you. We hear a lot about bonding nowadays. It is simply *the gluing of two objects together in a strong seal.* That about says it. As Genesis 2:24 declares, you two have been *glued together* by God Himself. Spiritual intimacy helps the glue to set.

3. ENDURANCE:

The third benefit you will receive from Spiritual intimacy is **endurance**. Your relationship will be able to endure time and trials because you and your mate are part of a *cord of three strands.*

4. SIGNIFICANCE:

And finally, you and your partner will come to know that you are significant. **Significance** is knowing that you have purpose in life, that you make a difference by being alive. Like Aquila and Priscilla, God has a job for you to do as a couple. You are important to His plan. We all need to feel significant, and Spiritual intimacy helps us realize that God has a **profound purpose in our marriage.**

C. How do you get it?

1. Definition of _____ -- A covenant is a binding agreement between two parties, like a contract. Your marriage itself is a covenant. And you and your wife or husband can make a covenant together concerning almost anything in your marriage.

2. A covenant includes a

_____ to accomplish your goal.

_____ to work the plan.

_____ to keep the covenant.

_____ to hold to agreement.

P O P A!

3. Why a Covenant? Luke 14:28-30 -- *Suppose one of you wants to build a tower. Will he not first sit down and estimate the cost to see if he has enough money to complete it? For if he lays the foundation and is not able to finish it, everyone who sees it will ridicule him, saying, 'This fellow began to build and was not able to finish.'*

4. **Example of covenants in Scripture:** 1 Samuel 18:3-4--*And Jonathan made a covenant with David because he loved him as himself. Jonathan took off the robe he was wearing and gave it to David, along with his tunic, and even his sword, his bow and his belt.*

5. **God expects us to keep our covenants/contracts** -- Numbers 30:2 --*When a man makes a vow to the LORD or takes an oath to obligate himself by a pledge, he must not break his word but must do everything he said.*

   Ecclesiastes 5:4,5--*When you make a vow to God, do not delay in fulfilling it. He has no pleasure in fools; fulfill your vow. It is better not to vow than to make a vow and not fulfill it.*

We know this is going to take effort on your part. But you know by now that worthwhile things **take effort**. If you're like the rest of us, you're already pummelled by demands on your time, emotions, mind and body. If you simply **add** Spiritual Intimacy **on top** of everything else in your life, it might slide off the pile, taking your determination to change with it.

If something 'has to give' in your busy life to allow room for you and your mate to start building Spiritual Intimacy together, we urge you to make that sacrifice and push something less critical aside. Then you will have room to make Spiritual Oneness the priority it should be. Choosing to grow together spiritually will enable you to bond closer as a couple than you ever dreamed possible. We sincerely pray that you and your spouse will choose to walk this Spiritual intimacy journey with us. It is worth it!

CHAPTER 11   SPIRITUAL INTIMACY

III. GROUP DISCUSSION QUESTIONS

1. What are some reasons why there are so few Christian couples who read the Bible and pray together regularly?

2. Give some examples of couples sharing a ministry together.

3. Relate an occasion when you experienced #4 (Shared faith in the tough times) and tell how it has strengthened your relationship.

4. Give some examples of covenants and evaluate each to see if they are POPA covenants.

CHAPTER 11 — SPIRITUAL INTIMACY

IV. COUPLE QUESTIONS

1. If you are not now reading and praying together regularly, then structure a Covenant to do so. Make sure you use all 4 elements (Plan, Obligation, Promise & Accountability).

2. If you are currently reading and praying together regularly, then structure a covenant around Shared Ministry. Again make sure you use all 4 elements (Plan, Obligation, Promise & Accountability).

Appendix A
MARRIAGE RELATIONSHIP EVALUATION

1. Common goals and values   1 2 3 4 5 6 7 8 9 10

2. Commitment to growth   1 2 3 4 5 6 7 8 9 10

3. Communication skills   1 2 3 4 5 6 7 8 9 10

4. Creative use of conflict   1 2 3 4 5 6 7 8 9 10

5. Appreciation and affection   1 2 3 4 5 6 7 8 9 10

6. Agreement on gender roles   1 2 3 4 5 6 7 8 9 10

7. Cooperation and teamwork   1 2 3 4 5 6 7 8 9 10

8. Sexual fulfillment   1 2 3 4 5 6 7 8 9 10

9. Money management   1 2 3 4 5 6 7 8 9 10

10. Parent effectiveness   1 2 3 4 5 6 7 8 9 10

Appendix B -- RECOMMENDED READING LIST

TITLE	AUTHOR
12 WAYS TO A BETTER MARRIAGE	Dr. Paul Mickey
199 QUESTIONS PARENTS ASK	Dr. Grace Ketterman
A GUIDE TO CHILD REARING	Dr. Bruce Narramore
AFTER EVERY WEDDING COMES A MARRIAGE	Florence Litauer
AS FOR ME AND MY HOUSE	Walter Wongerin Jr.
BARREN COUPLES BROKEN HEARTS	Alan & Patricia Trent
BECOMING ONE	Don Meredith
BEFORE YOU SAY "I DO"	Roberts & Wright
BEFORE YOU THROW IN THE TOWEL	Dr. Bob Moorehead
BELOVED UNBELIEVER	Jo Berry
BROKEN VOWS	Dr. Les Carter
BUILDING A GREAT MARRIAGE	Ann Ortland
CELEBRATION OF MARRIAGE	H. Norman Wright
CHRISTIAN LIVING IN THE HOME*	Jay Adams
CHRISTIAN PERSPECTIVES ON SEX & MARRIAGE	William Fitch
CLERGY COUPLES IN CRISIS	Dean Merrill
COMMUNICATION:KEY TO YOUR MARRIAGE*	H. Norman Wright
CREATIVE COUNTERPART	Linda Dillow
DARE TO DISCIPLINE*	James Dobson
DATING YOUR MATE	Bundschuh & Gilbert
DR. DOBSON ANSWERS YOUR QUESTIONS*	Dr. James Dobson
FAMILY BUILDING	Dr. George Rekers
FAMILY FORUM*	Jay Kessler
FIT TO BE TIED	Bill & Lynne Hybels
FOR BETTER OR BEST	Gary Smalley
FOR LOVERS ONLY	Stephen & Judith Schwanback
GAMES HUSBANDS & WIVES PLAY	John Drakeford
GETTING READY FOR MARRIAGE WORKBOOK	Hardin & Sloan
GOD'S PATTERN FOR THE HOME	Clarence Kerr
GOOD MARRIAGES TAKE TIME	David & Carole Hocking
GROWING A GREAT MARRIAGE	Bob & Emilie Barnes
HEDGES	Jerry Jenkins
HEIRS TOGETHER	Patricia Gundry
HIDE AND SEEK*	Dr. James Dobson
HIS NEEDS HER NEEDS	Willard Harley
HOLDING ON TO ROMANCE*	H. Norman Wright
HOW TO BE HAPPY THOUGH MARRIED	Tim La Haye
HOW TO HAVE A HAPPY MARRIAGE*	David & Vera Mace
HUSBANDS AND WIVES	William J. Peterson
I MARRIED YOU	Walter Trobisch
IF ONLY HE KNEW	Gary Smalley
IF ONLY YOU WOULD CHANGE	Luciano & Merris
IF TWO SHALL AGREE	Carey & Pamela Moore
INTENDED FOR PLEASURE*	Ed & Gaye Wheat
INTIMACY	Terry Hershey
INTIMACY TAPE SERIES*	Ed Wheat, M.D.
INTIMATE MARRIAGE	Charles M. Sell
LET'S MAKE A MEMORY*	Gaither & Dobson
LONELY HUSBANDS LONELY WIVES	Dennis Rainey
LOVE AND ANGER IN MARRIAGE*	David Mace
LOVE BUSTERS	Willard Harley
LOVE IS A DECISION*	Gary Smalley
LOVE MUST BE TOUGH*	Dr. James Dobson
MAKING CHILDREN MIND WITHOUT LOSING YOURS*	Dr. Kevin Leman
MARRIAGE DIVORCE REMARRIAGE IN THE BIBLE	Jay Adams
MARRIAGE SPIRITUALITY	Paul Stevens
MARRIED LOVERS, MARRIED FRIENDS*	Steve & Annie Chapman

TITLE	AUTHOR
MARRIED WITHOUT MASKS	Nancy Groom
MEN AND WOMEN*	Dr. Larry Crabb
MEN IN MIDLIFE CRISIS*	Jim Conway
PARENTS AND TEENAGERS*	Jay Kessler
PASSAGES OF MARRIAGE*	Minirth, Newman & Henfelt
PREPARING FOR ADOLESCENCE	Dr. James Dobson
PREPARING FOR YOUR MARRIAGE	William McRae
PREVENTING DIVORCE	McPherson & Biehl
PULLING TOGETHER WHEN YOU'RE PULLED APART*	Stuart & Jill Briscoe
RAISING GOOD CHILDREN	Dr. Thomas Lickona
RESOLVING CONFLICT IN MARRIAGE	Bob & Jan Horner
ROMANTIC LOVERS	David & Carole Hocking
SEASONS OF A MARRIAGE	Dr. Norm Wright
SECRET CHOICES*	Ed Wheat
SEX BEGINS IN THE KITCHEN*	Dr. Kevin Leman
SEX EDUCATION IS FOR THE FAMILY	Tim La Haye
SEX FOR CHRISTIANS	Lewis Smedes
SEX IS A PARENT AFFAIR	Letha Scanzoni
SEXUAL HAPPINESS IN MARRIAGE*	Herbert Miles
SIX KEYS TO A HAPPY MARRIAGE	Tim LeHaye
SO YOU'RE GETTING MARRIED	H. Norman Wright
SOLOMON ON SEX	Joseph Dillow
SOLVING MARRIAGE PROBLEMS	Jay E. Adams
STRAIGHT TALK TO MEN AND THEIR WIVES*	James Dobson
STRENGTHENING YOUR MATE'S SELF ESTEEM	Dennis & Barbara Rainey
STRIKE THE ORIGINAL MATCH*	Charles R. Swindoll
THE ACT OF MARRIAGE*	Tim & Beverly Lahaye
THE ART OF UNDERSTANDING YOUR MATE	Cecil Osborne
THE BATTLE FOR THE FAMILY	Tim La Haye
THE CHRISTIAN FAMILY	Larry Christenson
THE ENCYCLOPEDIA OF CHRISTIAN PARENTING	Leslie R. Keylock, Editor
THE FIRST YEARS OF FOREVER*	Ed Wheat
THE GIFT OF SEX*	Clifford & Joyce Penner
THE INTIMACY FACTOR	David & Jan Sloop
THE INTIMATE MARRIAGE*	Howard & Charlotte Clinebell
THE JOY OF COMMITTED LOVE	Gary Smalley
THE LANGUAGE OF LOVE*	Smalley & Trent
THE MARRIAGE BUILDER*	Lawrence J. Crabb, Jr.
THE MARRIAGE TRACK	Dave & Claudia Arp
THE MYTH OF THE GREENER GRASS	J. Allan Peterson
THE ROMANCE FACTOR*	Alan Loy Mc Ginnis
THE SECRET OF LOVING*	Josh Mc Dowell
THE SECRETS OF EFFECTIVE FATHERS	Ken Canfield
THREE SPEED DAD IN A TEN SPEED WORLD	Kel Groseclose
TO UNDERSTAND EACH OTHER*	Dr. Paul Tournier
TOGETHER AT HOME	Dean & Grace Merrill
TOWARD A GROWING MARRIAGE	Gary Chapman
VENTURES IN FAMILY LIVING	Roy B. Zuck
WHAT HUSBANDS WISH THEIR WIVES KNEW @ MONEY	Larry Burkett
WHAT LOVEMAKING MEANS TO A MAN*	Tim & Beverly LeHaye
WHAT LOVEMAKING MEANS TO A WOMAN*	Tim & Beverly LeHaye
WHAT WIVES WISH THEIR HUSBANDS KNEW @ WOMEN*	James Dobson
WHEN TWO WALK TOGETHER	Richard & Mary Strauss
WHERE HAVE ALL THE LOVERS GONE?	Pamala Condit Kennedy
WOMEN IN MIDLIFE CRISIS	Jim & Sally Conway
YOUR MARRIAGE IS GOD'S AFFAIR	Dwight Hervey Small

Note: * means it is recommended by GTO

Appendix C
RESOURCE ORDER FORM

ACHIEVING GOD'S DESIGN FOR MARRIAGE

1. **Leader's Guide** $24.95
2. **Couple's Guide** $10.00
3. **10 Couple's Guides** $100.00
    (1 additional **Couple's Guide** included)
4. **20 Couple's Guides** $200.00
    (1 **Leader's Guide** or 2 additional **Couple's Guides** included)
5. **Complete set of
    Overhead transparencies** $35.00
6. **Fill-in answers to blanks in Couple's Guide** .... N/C
7. **GTO FAMILY MINISTRIES Newsletter** .... N/C

Call us at 1-800-546-5486
or fill out the form below and mail it to:

> Harold or Bette Gillogly
> % GTO FAMILY MINISTRIES
> P.O. Box 1080
> Idyllwild, CA 92549

NAME: _____

STREET: _____

CITY: _____ **STATE:** ____ **ZIP:** _____

TELEPHONE # _____

ITEM # (s): _____ **QTY (s):** _____

Enclose check or money order for the appropriate amount to Harold or Bette Gillogly
(Book-Rate Shipping and handling are included -- call if you desire other shipping)
California residents please add Sales Tax